CRISIS IN BAGHDAD

"LEADERSHIP IN A RISK ADVERSE ENVIRONMENT"

By Colonel Gregory L. Marston (ret)

For my wife and family –
who supported me then and always will

TABLE OF CONTENTS

INTRODUCTION.. 4

CHAPTER ONE THE CHAVIS TURRET 14

CHAPTER TWO DIVERSION TO AFGHANISTAN...................................22

CHAPTER THREE BUILDING AN INTRODUCTORY BRIEFING TO INSTILL A WARRIOR MINDSET..31

CHAPTER FOUR BASE INSPECTION..39

CHAPTER FIVE FEEDING THE HUNGRY 44

CHAPTER SIX SECURITY BLACK HOLES AND BASE OPERATIONAL READINESS EXERCISES (ORES) "EYE OF THE HURRICANE" 50

CHAPTER SEVEN DRAINING THE USAF DUMPING GROUND – PERSONNEL ISSUES 75

CHAPTER EIGHT 'BIAP IS BAD' BRIEFING 87

CHAPTER NINE SAFEST BASE IN IRAQ..95

CHAPTER TEN REDESIGNING THE DANGEROUS TRAFFIC FLOW INTO BIAP AND OTHER AIR TRAFFIC SAFETY PROBLEMS...............99

CHAPTER ELEVEN MORALE BOOSTERS 107

CHAPTER TWELVE DEATH OF A TEAM 117

CHAPTER THIRTEEN AFTER THE DEPLOYMENT - SUICIDE OF A COMRADE 128

EPILOGUE 139

ACKNOWLEDGEMENTS..145

CRISIS IN BAGHDAD

"LEADERSHIP IN A RISK ADVERSE ENVIRONMENT"

INTRODUCTION

My purpose for this book is to provide a close look at combat leadership in an environment of risk aversion, that characterized the atmosphere when I arrived at Baghdad International Airport, Iraq in September, 2006. It was a time of great adversity in Iraq and was certainly a tipping point for the Second Iraq War (2003-Present). Baghdad, the capital city of Iraq, was an extremely dangerous place at the time with 50-90+ civilian murders occurring every single night during my tour. During that period, Sather Air Base, that I commanded, was subject to intermittent rocket attacks from that war-ravaged city.

This true tale is about making critical decisions that would reduce the potential for casualties. The issues that my staff and I discovered at Sather Air Base in our tour often had *not* been raised or addressed in over three and a half years of prior USAF commanders. Situations existed there, before my arrival, that could have caused harm or death to *hundreds* of Americans. The only reason that servicemen weren't killed previously, due to these unidentified problems, was just blind luck and/or the grace of God. Yet, it was a race against time to keep the enemy from discovering the weaknesses at this base and winning an easy propaganda victory that could turn possibly the war. This story is not about flying, combat or breaking down doors in Baghdad, but is about providing leadership, and encouraging it in subordinates in a combat environment at a forward deployment base in Southwest Asia.

While this book focuses on combat leadership issues, my intent is to demonstrate that *one person can make a difference*, especially when the path of least resistance would have been to do only the minimum required to make it through their tour. But, I am not about to present myself as a hero, because only those that have bled or died for their country can claim that right. Nor was it rough, because the Soldiers and Marines in the field had an infinitely tougher experience.

I had three jobs when I arrived in Iraq and they all centered around being a geographically separated commander in the USAF (U.S. Air Force). First, I was the base commander of Sather Air Base - the only USAF installation in the large Victory Base Complex (VBC). VBC was a tight group of large US Army camps, Sather Air Base, a prison, contractor operations, Iraqi Army and Air Force facilities on the outskirts of Baghdad. Sather Air Base was the main arrival and transit point for American troops and supplies into Iraq. On Sather, were a large number of Air Force personnel, some US Army people, British airmen and a few civilians.

My second job was to command the 447th Air Expeditionary Group (AEG). This group ran Sather Air Base and handled the many Air Force cargo aircraft and Army helicopters that came into the base every day. Finally, I was the senior airfield authority for BIAP (Baghdad International Airport). That meant that I was the military person who dealt with all the issues of Iraqi civilian-run Baghdad International Airport. All three of the jobs overlapped each other during the course of my tour in Iraq.

When I took this assignment, I had been promoted to Brigadier General, but had not been pinned on yet. The minimum risk path for me to ensure my promotion would have been to do as my predecessors had done, little or nothing and to "make no waves". However, when I volunteered for this last combat tour, I made the decision that I would give it my best effort and do what was right, regardless of how this would affect my future. I came to Iraq to help **win this war** and I did everything in my power to ensure that those under my command at Sather Air Base, Iraq, made it their top priority, also.

There is a popular misconception regarding military command, that it is just the simple act of the commander shouting orders to his/her people and then having them obeyed without question. In fact, from the outside, it may seem easy for a military commander to get his/her way by simply ordering one's followers toward a particular action. However, this is not the most effective way to lead. *The best leadership is to convince one's followers to take a particular course because it is in their best interest to do so.* Winning the argument and then leading from the front internalizes the way forward for the followers and gets the best participatory engagement. At times, I was forced to give lawful military orders and then to lead by example. But this was always a fallback position, as I usually tried to influence and sway my audience toward my way of thinking.

Writing about my Iraq experience details the biggest successes in my career, as well as my most significant failure. This dichotomy is still tough for me to comprehend, but I won't shirk from telling you the gritty details. I believe this book will show that we made substantial and critical changes to this hazardous base during our tour, often when previous administrations had done little or nothing to address alarming and grievous situations. However, long after the tour was over, the U.S. Air Force Inspector General (IG) would brand me as the worst sort of combat commander – a foul-mouthed, angry tyrant. This judgement was made by politically correct minions in air conditioned offices on the safety of U.S. soil, rather than by my commanders in Iraq or Al Udeid, Qatar. They ignored the many positive upgrades I instituted for the safety of my people and real efforts to make this tour the highlight of our airmen's lives. They simply labeled me as a bully and a despot which prevented me from receiving the promotion for which I had worked for over 28 years to achieve.

For a time during the wars in Afghanistan and Iraq, U.S. Air Force (USAF) Group Commander positions could be filled by senior positions in the Air National Guard (ANG) or Air Force Reserve Command (AFRC) ranks. It was in that capacity that I served my last two combat tours as a USAF, active duty, commander. This was a great opportunity, but also a huge challenge, since my full-time job was as an American Airlines Boeing 777 Captain flying out of New York City.

I had plenty of experience in combat zones during my ANG career, holding leadership roles in three previous combat tours to Southwest Asia. I had been the Operations Officer for an A-10 "Warthog" deployment to Kuwait for Operation SOUTHERN WATCH in 1995. I was the Squadron Commander of that same A-10 ANG unit for a similar deployment to Kuwait in 1999. In 2002-2003, I served as the Group Commander who commanded the entire airfield, all USAF personnel and an A-10 group at Bagram Air Base, Afghanistan.

During these three Southwest Asia tours, I flew 80 A-10A combat missions. While it may seem unusual for a Traditional Guardsman (the term for a part-time person in the National Guard) to have the ability to serve in leadership positions of authority in combat, for the typical Guardsman, both aircrew and aircraft maintainers, it was normal to serve 100-120 work days per year in his fighter squadron. This was the only way to stay proficient in today's complex aircraft and tactics. It was certainly an all-consuming, but exciting "part-time" job and entailed much more than just the "one weekend a month" commitment that the public imagines we serve. In fact, because many Guardsmen stay with their units and weapons systems for many years, their experience level often exceeds that of their active duty counterparts who move to other assignments every 2-3 years.

From 2004 to 2006, I was the 111th Fighter Wing Commander for the ANG A-10 wing at Willow Grove Air Reserve Station, Pennsylvania. It was rather unusual for a Traditional Guardsman to be given the honor of being a fighter wing commander, and had only happened a few times in the 90-year history of this storied unit. Unfortunately, my tour as Wing Commander was marred by the Base Closure and Realignment Commission (BRAC) decision to close our base and our unit. Out of roughly 90 or so ANG wings across America, the 111th Fighter Wing was *the only unit specifically scheduled for closure* by the 2005 commission. I spent most of my time as wing commander trying to help my unit and its 1,100 members to escape being axed by BRAC. My decision to volunteer for a tour in Iraq was an attempt to end my combat career on a positive note, despite the relentless negative atmosphere created by the BRAC's arbitrary decision. Although I took a *huge pay cut* to deploy to Iraq (airline pay versus military pay) I felt compelled to do so. My successors eventually saved the 111th Wing but at the price of losing our A-10s in 2010. Today it is a highly successful MQ-9 "Reaper" drone wing.

I noticed two things when I arrived at VBC. First was the wet blanket of a "do the minimum to survive the tour" mentality that seemed to permeate the US Army leadership strata. There were roughly 60,000 Army troops at VBC and they seemed to have little to do except exist. I picked this up during my initial introduction to the nine mess halls throughout VBC, where I talked to many of these troops. I do not fault these soldiers or their leadership up to the Colonel (O-6) level. Those below the O-6 level, especially in the Army, follow the will of their commanders. There were over 30 generals in Iraq and that number seemed excessive to me versus previous wars. Secondly, it also became blatantly obvious to me, shortly after my arrival, that we were *losing this war* and the effort to stabilize Baghdad. I specifically recall an intelligence figure during our weekly staff meeting in October, 2006 that there were **93 civilian murders in _one_ 24-hour period in Baghdad**. This was not an unusual number for this metropolis at that time. For a city, with 6 million residents, with more people than Los Angeles this amount of crime and hatred could not be endured for very long. The forces of discord and mayhem were winning easily against an American leadership that largely wanted to 'cruise through their tour'. Those at the top either did not know that we were losing or were only concerned with minimizing its fallout during their tour. I know this because, when I briefed the civilian leadership in Baghdad on the more negative aspects of the security situation around Sather and the Iranian influx of weapons, they were shocked at what I had to say.

I grew up during the Vietnam War. During my time as a cadet at the U.S. Air Force Academy (1974-78), almost all of my instructors there had been Air Force pilots flying in that very divisive conflict. I heard the frustration from these officers who fought bravely (some were even Prisoners of War – POW) and whose sacrifices were rendered futile by numerous U.S. political and military mistakes.

As a cadet and young Air Force officer, **I saw the U.S. military at its nadir**, perhaps the lowest it has been anytime in American history. Many Vietnam veterans, upon returning to the U.S., were actually spit on and cursed by civilians after spending a year fighting that war. These same veterans, whether involuntarily drafted or volunteers, were somehow blamed for the colossal errors committed far above their rank during its duration. The top U.S. television show of the day ("MASH") largely portrayed the military as a bunch of buffoons. The typical American TV drama of that era usually had the bad guy as a drugged-out and/or murderous Vietnam veteran. It took almost two decades for the military to extract itself from this dark place. One way the military did this was to take a long, honest look at the Vietnam War and the many mistakes made there. Later as an Air Force and Air Guard officer, I took officer training courses, termed Professional Military Education, or PME, as my rank increased. To its credit, this curriculum spent much time dissecting the Vietnam fiasco. From the strategic level on down there were many blunders made in this conflict. Those that wrote these military histories did not "sugar coat" these errors, but discussed them in great detail. Once the young officers of Vietnam became the commanding generals in the Wars of the Sand (starting in 1990), there was a definite effort to correct some of the most egregious mistakes of Vietnam. This presented new issues but at least solved some of the big problems at a personal level, such as the ban on drinking (and drug use) while serving in predominantly Muslim combat areas. Also, after Vietnam, there was a premium placed on realistic training for all the services, including combined forces exercises. Personally, I looked at the issues of Iraq (and in Afghanistan where I served in 2002-3) through the prism of Vietnam and promised myself - "never again". You can avoid mistakes in the future by learning from the errors of the past. I swore that I would use what I had learned from the Vietnam War, and my own combat experience, to make sure we did not repeat mistakes. Sadly, I saw some of the same leadership oversights from Vietnam repeated in Iraq. I hope that this book will inspire a new set of leaders to learn from *our* successes and mistakes to propel us forward in the continuing wars in the deserts and beyond.

The history of Iraq, for our purposes here, begins in 1979 when Saddam Hussein became the dictator of Iraq. A despot, who modeled himself after Joseph Stalin, Saddam took the vast oil wealth of his nation and spent it on himself, his tribe, and military hardware for war. Saddam started a horrific conflict, resulting in hundreds of thousands of casualties, with Iran from 1980-88. That war ended in a muddled fashion at the end of that decade with Iraq hugely in debt. Saddam had even used toxic chemical weapons against the Iranians and the Kurds in his own country in that conflict.

In August 1990, Saddam invaded Kuwait. This invasion was largely a money grab to pay off his huge war debts. He was famously driven out of Kuwait by the U.S. and its massive international coalition in Operation DESERT STORM in 1991. After DESERT STORM Saddam continued to live in luxury in his many palaces, while his people suffered under the United Nation embargos of the 1990's. Because of Iraqi operations against the Kurds and the Shias and his non-compliance with United Nation resolutions, US fighters and bombers began overflights of Iraq, beginning in the early 1990's until 2003. My own A-10 ANG wing deployed to Kuwait for these patrol missions over Iraq in 1995, 1999 and 2001. The overflight sorties of Iraq were called Operations PROVIDE COMFORT, SOUTHERN WATCH and NORTHERN WATCH. By 2003 the conflict between the U.S. and Iraq had extended over three U.S. Presidential terms and had reached critical mass. The question was should our nation stop the patrol missions and end sanctions?

This prior history may be why we invaded Iraq in 2003. Although the reasons for the invasion may provide for a good debate, they will not be covered extensively in this book. For us in the military, this was an academic question. We went where our civilian leaders told us to go. When we invaded Iraq (which occurred while I was commanding in Afghanistan) many of my friends and comrades in the A-10 pilot community were already flying missions directly supporting the Army, the Marines and the UK Army in Iraq. After we had conquered Iraq in just 22 days, in one of the quickest invasions in American history, the story gets cloudier. We did not find the weapons of mass destruction we thought were there and the U.S. leadership then made a series of strategic blunders.

The biggest overall mistake, in my opinion, was in not resurrecting the Iraqi military using the soldiers and NCOs who had served in it before. By bypassing this group of old warriors, we made instant enemies of hundreds of thousands of those that no longer had a purpose in life. Many that we fought in later years were simply troops that wanted a job and knew where all the old caches of weapons were stored. The rockets and mortar shells that hit Sather Air Base often were fired by the soldiers that we had left behind in the aftermath of the invasions. Another error was the glacial pace in rebuilding the Iraqi Army and Air Force after the invasion. For instance, by late 2006 there were *only three aircraft* in the entire Iraqi Air Force, all stationed at New Al Muthana Iraqi Air Base (which was right next to Sather Air Base). This was from an Air Force that had operated hundreds of aircraft in the Saddam Hussein days. The very slow growth of the Iraqi forces was a result of top-down American leadership decisions. There was no reward for helping the Iraqi armed forces to train or improve their operations and little return for a commander who gave this kind of assistance.

In my time at Sather Air Base I challenged every commander in my Group to work closely with their nearby Iraqi Air Force counterparts and they did so magnificently. Still it took new American civilian and military leadership in 2007 (Secretary of Defense Gates and General Petraeus) to change the path away from the failures of the previous few years in Iraq.

For the U.S. military in 2006, the official answer to why we were in Iraq was to establish a democratic Arab country that had known only tyranny before. I saw a rich oil nation that had been run for the pleasure of one man, Saddam Hussein. I visited many of the 50-plus palaces that Saddam built for himself throughout the land. The Victory Base complex, a collection of US Army, Iraqi, US Air Force and contractor camps, started simply as the huge enclosed compound of palaces used by Saddam and his family during his long, bloody reign. All of those palaces now were taken over by US forces. For instance, my domed headquarters at Sather Air Base was referred to as the "Glass House" and was the former VIP lounge for Saddám's airport visitors. The daughter of Saddam had her own palace, now located in VBC, which was used as an Air Force headquarters.

American forces had rebuilt other nations after defeating authoritarian dictatorships in prior wars. I had visited the bases in Germany, Japan and even spent a year protecting South Korea in 1982 (over 29 years after the war ended there). By 2006, the Iraqi people had already enthusiastically voted in three separate free elections in that country. My goal for Iraq was to try to continue building the fragile democracy that had taken hold there and to help get the Iraqi forces, specifically the Iraqi Air Force, ready to take over for us in the future.

What did I expect to find when I arrived at Sather Air Base and the 447th Group? I honestly thought that most of the problems had been fixed and that it would be a smoothly running operation. The base had been there for three and a half years and about 14 commanders had proceeded me. I believed that, at most, I might have one or two issues to mend. I had seen the huge amount of progress that we made at Bagram Air Base, Afghanistan during my previous deployment in 2002-2003. Bagram at that time was like the Wild West and its problems were immense. That is because Afghanistan was newly conquered and Bagram Air Base, a base built by the Soviets, was itself largely destroyed and poorly constructed and maintained to begin with. That base was located in a windy, snowy bowl surrounded by the high mountains of the Hindu Kish. Still, during my tour at Bagram I was able to begin the process of moving personnel from tents to wooden huts. I had revamped the unruly air traffic patterns over Bagram. Finally, I worked with the Army to personally design and gain approval for a new $100 million base and runway plan. These were just the highlights of the many issues solved during my time at Bagram Air Base. Furthermore, Afghanistan was a desperately poor fifth world nation that had suffered both Soviet occupation and Taliban rule.

Iraq to me was another story. It was an oil rich nation that had tapped European building firms to build first-class structures and runways. Sather Air Base was formerly part of the large Baghdad International Airport (BIAP), the only civilian airfield servicing Baghdad itself. The airport structures and runway there were well built and sturdy. The problems at Sather and BIAP were not with the initial construction, but rather the neglect, apathy and a past attitude of "doing it the way it had been done before". That mentality would change with my arrival.

My overall objective while serving in Iraq was to accomplish our mission and to help WIN THE WAR. It was easy in the dust, confusion and every day crisis management to forget that purpose. It was easy in the dust, confusion and every day crisis management to forget that purpose.Some leaders who came there were only concerned with performing just at a level sufficient to earn a medal or to be able to list Iraq as an accomplishment.

But, our mission was to win this war and nothing should ever come in the way of that objective. That didn't mean that I was going to ask my people to take unnecessary risks. Even dangerous jobs such as explosive ordnance disposal (EOD) must be done in a safe manner. Once, I had delayed the Secretary of State from landing for

30 minutes, due to an IED threat; I wasn't trying to cover my butt, but rather to be sure that the enemy forces weren't about to launch a clever attack on such a high value target.

So, throughout my tour, I simply asked myself whether my actions or those of my group were going to help us win the war or not. It was a basic guidepost for my actions throughout my tour and served me well in my decision making.

I'm not saying that I had it all right or that I was the only one who saw the immense problems in Iraq and, specifically, in the Baghdad area in 2006-7. The subsequent surge in Iraq in the Spring of 2007 was a massive step in the right direction which eventually won the war there. The political armistice with the Sunni tribes in 2007 could have been done far sooner. But I know that, at my level, I was one of the first to light the candle of change in Iraq. I was in a unique position to do something in Iraq and did so. That is what this book is about – making a difference in a sea of apathy.

Yet, I made many mistakes. My intense energy and quick temper were known to those who dealt with me in Iraq. I attempted to mentor whoever I could in Iraq, but I did not suffer fools. We were at war in Iraq and people's lives were at stake. I was there to fix problems, as this book will show, and my previous experiences in Kuwait, Afghanistan and as an A-10 Wing, Group and Squadron Commander were my guide. As one of the most experienced commanders in Iraq (Active Duty or ANG), it was my primary goal to help us win this war. No person or obstacle was going to stand in my way of making that happen. But there was a price to be paid for my fierce purpose. This book will highlight the successes and failures of my mission. I write this now with the perspective of another decade of my life. I'm telling this tale as honestly as I can and hope that you find it as exciting as when I lived it.

CHAPTER ONE
THE CHAVIS TURRET

"Airmen Helping Airmen using Yankee Ingenuity"

This is a story of turning a tragedy into a lifesaving improvement for future airmen, by virtue of personal initiative and ingenuity. This incident began very early in my tour in September 2006 and is an example of the law of unintended consequences. During this time of the Iraq War, small Air Force units were deployed all over the country to augment the U.S. Army. This was an attempt to help the Army, which was over-stretched at the time. These isolated Air Force units were given the unusual name of "In Lieu of" Airmen.

These "in lieu of" squadrons were often deployed far away from the main Air Force bases in Iraq. All of these units were headquartered at Balad Air Base and worked under the command of Brigadier General (BG) Robin Rand. BG Rand was the overall commander of all U.S. Air Force units and personnel in Iraq. However, the problem for these small units was that they had no mid-level officers between General Rand and their much lower ranked commanders, who were usually Captains or Majors. Thus, these "in lieu of" units had little or no officer "top cover". They were like a lion pride with no male lion king.

Very early in my tour we were contacted by one such forlorn unit – the 732nd Expeditionary Security Forces Squadron (732nd ESFS), a small security forces (military police) squadron working in Baghdad with the Army. This unit augmented the Army and Iraqi police forces patrolling the unsafe streets of Baghdad. Their HMMWV (High Mobility Multipurpose Wheeled Vehicle or **Humvee**) vehicles had been provided by the Army and were generally in poor shape (i.e., their Army counterparts had given them some of their worst vehicles).

Theoretically BG Rand was their boss, so I was under no obligation to help this squadron. Regardless, I immediately enlisted my Chief of Maintenance, CMSgt. (Chief Master Sergeant) Rossi to do whatever we could to help this unit. We **adopted** them because it was the right thing to do, even though it increased our vehicle maintenance workload. Their Humvees were in terrible condition; including some that still had unrepaired shrapnel or bullet damage! They had received no periodic repairs or any other type of maintenance in a long time. We began to address that immediately, although it definitely took some time to get their Humvees back up to a reasonable state of functionality. We continued to help this unit for the rest of my tour.

This unit suffered a tragedy on October 14, 2006. While on patrol in Baghdad one of their machine gunners, Airman First Class (A1C) Leebenard "Lee" Chavis was killed in action (KIA) by a sniper while manning his .50 Caliber machine gun. The gunner sits or stands in a hole in the ceiling of the HMMWV, with only a small frontal armor plate for protection. *This shooting was a preventable tragedy*, as you will see.

Before the memorial ceremony for Airman Chavis, BG Rand came to Baghdad to get a briefing from the unit's commander. Rand brought me with him to this depressing meeting. The unit's commander was justifiably proud of his units' activities in Baghdad during the previous months, but gave us a bleak picture of the many challenges they faced, complete with graphic photographs. Religious in-fighting between Sunnis and Shiites (factions of the Moslem religion) in Baghdad had reached epic proportions by the fall of 2006. During Saddam Hussein's time as dictator of Iraq, 1979-2003, his political and security forces, comprised predominantly of Sunnis, played all the various ethnic, tribal, political and religious factions against each other. But mainly he conspired against the Shias and the Kurds, going so far as to use chemical weapons against the Kurds in the city of Halabja in March of 1988. During my A-10 "Thunderbolt II" Operation SOUTHERN WATCH tour in 1995, Hussein was pumping water out of the marshes on the lower Euphrates River to denigrate the habitat of the Shiite "Marsh Arabs" so his forces could engage them more effectively. We watched helplessly from above in our "Warthog" aircraft as Saddam used environmental warfare against his own people.

After the fall of Saddam Hussein in 2003, the various religious groups began to form militias to take revenge on each other for the years of depredations against them. By our time, civilians were being murdered in the most gruesome manner possible in Baghdad and then dumped in the streets to be discovered by passing U.S. Army, U.S. Air Force and Iraqi police patrols in their Humvees. The photographs told the horrible tale. Civilians were being shot, bludgeoned, garroted, power-drilled into bones, burned with blow-torches, etc. – all inflicted in a manner to cause the maximum amount of pain and suffering to the victim before their deaths. Patrols of this small Air Force unit alone had recovered *over 600 bodies*, during their tour of duty. Although they were an Air Force police unit, the conditions in Baghdad were too dangerous for them to perform any investigation into these hideous murders. It was during one of these patrols when Chavis was hit. He was in a very vulnerable position because his Humvee was parked for an extended period while other members of his patrol recovered bodies. At that time, the top gunner position only had a small frontal shield on their beat-up Army Humvees.

Besides the tragedy of losing a fellow Airmen in Baghdad to sniper fire, I worried about the post-traumatic stress disorder (PTSD) that these young men and women would face when this nightmare was over and they returned home. Based on the horrific color pictures of the Iraqi victims I can only imagine what they had seen in person, day after day. My immediate concern was how we could further help this unit *now*. I personally vowed to do anything to assist these embattled airmen from this small unit in Baghdad.

After the briefing for BG Rand and myself, we then attended the memorial ceremony for A1C Chavis. I had about 20-30 people from my unit at Sather for this service and overall there were about 100 persons at the observance. A1C Lee Chavis had been raised in Hampton, Virginia, and was from a military family. The ceremony went very well with the speakers including his commander and his non-commissioned officer (NCO). However, it was Chavis's best friend who really made an impression on me. This friend had grown up with Lee Chavis. He remembered Chavis as a rambunctious young man who was well liked by his friends, comrades and supervisors. The most stirring part of this friend's tale was the fact that Chavis had twice given away *all* of his earthly possessions to his friends. The first time in Virginia and then again, just weeks before his death. He had had some sort of premonition about his upcoming death, yet continued to do his duty to the end. As I heard this stirring part of his young friend's story, I began to formulate a plan in my head.

When we got on the bus to go back to Sather, I again talked to Chief Rossi, my NCO in charge of vehicle maintenance. I told Rossi that I wanted him to contact this unit's Security Forces commander the next day and for the two of them to design a new, upgraded gun turret for their HMMWVs. This commander was to tell Rossi what the gun turret position needed and then he was to design and build a prototype. Once built, they would then test the design model on the streets of Baghdad. Rossi and I agreed that he would assign three Airmen from his maintenance crew, whose sole purpose was to build this turret. Work was to begin at once and I left it up to Rossi, who was from own Air National Guard unit, to handle the details of this project.

The really unsettling thing about Humvee gun turrets in Iraq was that, after three and a half years of war, there was no standardization of their design either for Army or Air Force vehicles. In the famous battle of Mogadishu, Somalia in 1993, unarmored Humvees were ripped apart by small arms fire in the urban warfare of the "Blackhawk Down" incident. Yet, these same vehicle types were operating in Baghdad a decade later with the same vulnerabilities.

Fortunately, after service and congressional complaints reached the Secretary of Defense early in the Iraqi War, the original thin-skinned Humvee design began being modified by "Up Armor" kits of armor plating and ballistic glass. By 2006, all Humvees in Iraq were on the fourth up-armored version, and with each new design, the walls and ballistic glass were getting thicker and thicker. But, in contrast to the new upgraded armor, the gun turret remained a haphazard mixture of designs with the USAF (U.S. Air Force) model being the worst and least protected version in theater. The Air Force design had the gunners' whole head and upper torso exposed above the turret in all quadrants (see photograph). I became a student of all the turret designs in Iraq and was shocked by the lack of cover and standardization for the gunner position. We determined that were going to fix it for this security forces unit, with the hope that it would be adopted by other Air Force units in Iraq.

I maintained a close watch on our turret design through my weekly staff meetings and by visits to the new maintenance building to see how the work was progressing. I was extremely proud of Rossi and his three Airmen, because they were obviously putting their maximum effort into this project. CMSgt Rossi had a brilliant idea, which was to go to the Army vehicle junkyard in Baghdad and cannibalize thick, bulletproof armor from battle-damaged or wrecked up-armored Humvees. The use of scrap material reduced the delay in procuring the materials while keeping the price of his design to just $1000! Just about the time we started the turret design project, the Army issued a video concerning the recent upturn in sniper activity in Baghdad and how to counter this dangerous threat. Besides using bulletproof materials to provide protection from small caliber weapons, it was also important to camouflage the gunner to the maximum extent possible. So, we incorporated all this information into our new turret design.

Rossi and his team came out with the first prototype in just *48 days*. In honor of A1C Chavis's sacrifice, I decided to name it the "Chavis turret". Much of the design was predicated on the scrap armor plating, referred to as Armox, and ballistic glass that the Rossi's airmen had gotten out of the Army junk yard. Version 1 of the Chavis turret had a large front plate of heavy-duty Armox with two large ballistic glass windows incorporated in it for seeing out the front. The front panel and the sides extended well over the head of the gunner. The entire back of the rotatable turret was covered with protective Kevlar plating. Directly behind the gunner was a small window of ballistic glass and that had "Chavis Turret" painted on the outside. The top of the turret was open to the sky but covered with a camo netting so no one could see into the turret from above. Finally, this turret came in under the maximum weight for a roof turret for the Humvee. I was very proud of the Version 1 turret that Rossi and his team had created. It was delivered on Dec 2, 2006 and we began testing the model at Sather Air Base six days later, using it for patrolling around the base.

What were the improvements of the Chavis turret over the earlier USAF gun turret design? There was a vast increase in the amount of shielding in all directions; it provided 360 degrees of protection for the gunner. Not only were the sides and back of the gunner covered in this new turret, but also the *height* of the shielding was greatly increased (well over the top of the gunner's head). Remember that A1C Chavis was shot because his head was not protected by armor or ballistic glass. The Chavis Turret was a remarkable feat of Yankee ingenuity that had been designed and fabricated in under two months, for very little money. Upon the rollout of the version 1 turret, I presented a commander's challenge coin to reward each of the three builders and Chief Rossi, honoring them for providing a wonderful holiday gift for the combat-tested members of the security forces squadron.

I believe in my own slogan, "Don't fall in love with your own design". After the roll out, it was now time to test and get feedback on the version 1 turret. We began testing the turret around Sather. We also took the Chavis turret to U.S. Army Command Sergeant Majors Bean and Mellinger of the Multi-National Corps Iraq (MNC-I). Both were experts in turret design and Bean had survived *seven* improvised explosive devises (IEDs) – booby trap explosions in Up-Armored Humvees.

They began by giving us feedback on our turret and showed us where the US Army was going with their own new turret designs. Both immediately stated that there was a design flaw in the Chavis turret version 1. The large front plate hung over the forward edge of the roof of the Humvee. If there was an IED explosion in the front of the Humvee, the Chavis turret's frontal armor would funnel the hot gases right into the gunners' face. It was flaw that had to be fixed.

We also had a chance to examine the U.S. Army's new turret design. It was an 800-lb. monster that needed hydraulic power to turn the turret (our Chavis turret was human powered). According to Rossi, this also put the U.S. Army test turret in Iraq at over 400 pounds heavier than the maximum weight for the Humvee roof. The Army's prototype turret, plus the latest Up-Armored Humvee armor, now placed this test vehicle over *2400 pounds in excess of the maximum weight* of the Hummer chassis, which would have major effects on the vehicles suspension and stability, as well as on the maintenance requirements to keep them running. To my mind this was not a sustainable vehicle for long-term use in combat.

After meeting with the Command Sergeant Majors of MNCI, I felt for a short time that we were wasting our time and that our turret building program was way over our heads. Yet upon further reflection, it was clear that Rossi and his team had delivered a turret that corrected the main design flaws of the old USAF turret. In addition, it was done for a pittance compared to its competitors and under the maximum weight tolerances for the Humvee. So, I had Rossi immediately begin fixing the IED issues of the version 1 design and also to provide more ballistic windows for improved gunner field of view. Meanwhile, we continued to display the version 1 model to anyone who was interested in seeing it. When Fox News Correspondent Lieutenant Colonel, (LtCol, retired), Oliver North came through Sather, we showed him the turret. He was impressed and took pictures and video of the turret. The most effective exhibition, however, was for the Central Command Air Force (CENTAF) Commander, Lt General Gary North.

This was General North's second visit to Sather Air Base during my command. The primary purpose of this visit was to officially open the new Air Force DFAC (chow hall) at Sather on Christmas night. Although we all had to wear body armor for the visit, based on my assessment of the threat level at Sather over Christmas, it was still a really good holiday. General North and I were going to christen the dining hall together (I named it the 'TSgt Walter M. Moss Jr Airpower DFAC').

Before the ceremony, I briefed General North on our development of the Chavis turret. He was very impressed with our ingenuity, foresight and attempt to standardize the gun turret position for the USAF combat ones in Iraq and Afghanistan. During the briefing, he asked me if we could construct more Chavis turrets at Sather AB. I told him we could, if he could assign us seven full-time welders and give us additional funding. Gently, he said that it was ridiculous to build turrets at a combat location when he had hundreds of personnel to do it at the quiet base camp of Al Udeid AB, Qatar. So, we gave the latest drawings of version 2 turret (still in production) to General North and Colonel Jolivette, CENTAF Director of Force Protection, for their use. General North gave CENTAF commanders' challenge coins to reward each of the Chavis building team, including Chief Rossi. They certainly deserved it. The challenge coins were large, specially-made medallions which usually had the presenter's rank pictured visually on one half the coin and on the other side his/her job title, often in very ornate fashion. Ornamentation and uniqueness generally increased with the rank of the giver. They were a highly sought after form of immediate recognition for superior service. Everyone liked to receive challenge coins.

On Jan 5, 2007, the **Chavis Turret Version 2** was delivered to the Security Forces Squadron for testing in Baghdad. The turret had now entered the big time. The second turret fixed the IED issue. It was not a perfect design, but it was a vast improvement over the previous ones. The airmen were very excited to test this new prototype. If this turret saved even one life, then the ingenuity, effort and dogged determination to create it would have all been worth it!

After the 447th AEG change out of personnel and leadership from Sather AB in late January 2007, Colonel Gerard Jolivette's own team at Al Udeid took the Sather turret version 2 plans and started working with the Air Force Security Forces Force Protection Battlelab in the United States for the next version of the Chavis turret. As with our Sather versions, they used pre-existing Humvee armor. They also added a top to the turret. The Chavis turret Version 3 from Al Udeid AB, Qatar came out in March 2007. Later that year, the new Chavis turret became the standardized turret for all the USAF combat vehicles in Iraq and Afghanistan (over 60 vehicles). What started with a tragedy for a young airman on the streets of Baghdad unleashed a tag team of hard working maintenance and design personnel in the 447th AEG and at the Air Force Security Forces Battlelab. It was a use of Yankee engineering and ingenuity, using scrap or cannibalized materials from wrecked vehicles and a desire to save lives that gave us the standardized Chavis turret for Iraq and Afghanistan. It was airmen helping airmen in the best sense of the word!

CHAPTER TWO
DIVERSION TO AFGHANISTAN

My trip to get to Iraq ended up being a long and convoluted one. I departed out of Philadelphia and proceeded to NAS Norfolk, Virginia where I spent a short night. While waiting to board the civilian charter airliner for Qatar I was sent to the VIP lounge and told that they would give me the first chance to board the aircraft. By mistake or design the Navy personnel waited until the aircraft was almost full before coming to get me out of this gilded cage. By that time, all of the bigger first class seats were filled and I was forced to sit in the middle of several enlisted troops at the back of the aircraft for the long flight. Not a problem, except, as the ranking member of the flight I was the "Troop Commander" for the flight and every time there was a passenger issue, I had to get out of my seat to deal with it.

Many hours later we deplaned on the ramp in Qatar in the 110-120° F midday heat (43-48°C). That was the beginning of what is usually described in the military parlance as a "goat rope". Which is to say, mass confusion and little, if any, organization. The Air Force passenger terminal personnel treated us like we were their worst enemies. We were all herded into a hot, humid room without air conditioning and broken into sections based on our scheduled destination base. Once again, I was designated the troop commander of all the passengers going to Baghdad International Airport (BIAP) the next day. As I had done on the aircraft I immediately established an officer as my second-in-command, and designated several non-commissioned officers (NCO's = senior enlisted personnel) for various jobs such as "head counts", "water bottle retrieval" and "medical assistance". These functions proved essential for the fiasco that we were about to endure. After getting everyone in our BIAP section assembled, we were directed back to the oven-hot flight line (where temperatures were 20-30°F *warmer* on the concrete ramp) to sort our bags from the mountain of several hundred bags piled near the aircraft. First, we all had to find our bags and then bring out certain clothing and body armor needed for the next day or two, information that should have been provided before we departed.

It was a complete debacle. Of course, the people at Qatar could have told everyone about this required gear *before we packed*, but they didn't do that, so everyone was forced to do it on an open concrete ramp in a $120°+$ environment. After two hours on the oven-like flight line sorting bags and clothes, some people started to collapse from the heat. Only then did the terminal support personnel give the impression that they cared. This may seem like a crazy way to sort out bags, but the Al Udeid passenger terminal service NCOs and officers conveyed an impression of indifference. The passenger and arrival personnel simply treated all their fellow airmen like cattle. I'm a professional airline pilot and I've seen thousands of terminal operations. Our experience at Al Udeid was like dealing with the world's worst airline personnel. This was a little surprising since it was one of the easiest bases at which to work. No shelling's from rockets and mortars, no breakneck schedule, no requirement to wear body armor and ice cold beer every night. We called Al Udeid "Camp Cupcake" because it was such an easy assignment. Yet, the leaders there had evidently not instilled a sense of purpose or mission in their personnel. Incidentally, about a month after this event, the commander at Al Udeid AB issued a formal apology to the entire Central Command area for their disorganized, poor handling and treatment of all the passengers going through their hub base. Fortunately, I'd been through this drill before and no one from our section fainted as we assigned work schedules and water breaks in the monstrous heat. After such a long flight, followed by hours of working outside in the heat, I was ready to get into an air-conditioned tent. By the time my section had arrived at the area to receive our tent assignment I felt like our troop leaders had finally created order from the enforced chaos of the bag sorting. But right as we were about to go to our air-conditioned rest tent, I received a message stating that Lieutenant General (LtGen - 3-star general) North wanted to see *me* as soon as possible. As the Joint Force Air Component Commander (JFACC) for all the CENTCOM air forces he was the top Air Force commanding general overseeing Iraq and Afghanistan. Thus, I was a little surprised by this call. His driver arrived shortly to pick me up with my newly found bags and we proceeded toward the Central Command Air Force (CENTAF) Headquarters.

The messenger wanted to take me directly to see Lt Gen North, but after the last 20 hours of transit and arrival activities, I insisted on 30-second shower and a change into a clean uniform before the meeting.

I made it just in time for my appointment. I was first introduced to Major General (Maj Gen) Holland, the Deputy Commander for CENTAF, who was reviewing my military biography when I arrived. He asked me if I'd heard any news in the last two days. I told him I hadn't. He told me that there had been a friendly fire incident, officially termed "fratricide", in Afghanistan, involving an A-10 'Warthog' and Canadian troops and that I had been selected to be the interim Board of Inquiry president. One Canadian soldier had been killed in the incident, bad enough in itself, but made worse by the fact that he was a Canadian hero, a gold medal winner in the Olympics. In addition, 33 other Canadians had been wounded in the incident. Besides being a horrible tragedy, it was also a public relations disaster.

What is a fratricide incident? It's when an allied weapons system, such as an aircraft, tank or soldier, mistakenly targets and attacks its own forces. Fratricide is endemic to the history of warfare, going back to the most ancient historical accounts. It has been estimated that, historically, 10-15% of all combat casualties were committed by their own forces. In combat, the action if often fast and furious with events happening quickly and often with less than optimum visual cues or communications. Judgements often have to be made in a split-second, based sometimes on incomplete or erroneous information, with the pull of a gun trigger or the swing of a sword (in ancient times) having instant and deadly results. In modern warfare, increased speed and longer distances challenge the maximum limits of our sensors or the human eye. All American military personnel train hard to eliminate fratricide, but it is still very easy to commit. I myself have made mistakes in training, when we were just using non-lethal or simulated weapons. Real combat includes Clausewitz's "fog of war", quick decision-making in real-time, genuine weapons and actual troops, all of which makes it a dangerous and often a confusing environment.

The A-10 community was very familiar with friendly fire incidents. Not because they were so numerous but because our primary mission was supporting ground forces, either our own (like the Army or Marines) or our allies. Whenever you have to employ weapons in close proximity to friendly forces, fratricide is a constant threat. Our goal in the A-10 was to never have a friendly fire incident. Yet, it didn't matter how many tens of thousands of successful combat missions are conducted, with often just yards separating the enemy and our forces, people only seemed to remember when an A-10 had killed our own or allied soldiers.

I was proud of my achievements during my tour at Bagram Air Base, Afghanistan in 2002-2003 but my best was commanding a forward-located combat base and an A-10 group that flew 1600 combat missions with *no* fratricide incidents – either for our own troops or Afghan civilians (including 54 combat missions myself). So, the friendly fire incident in Afghanistan, that I was to investigate, was a huge, serious problem, one that demanded an inquiry. I was pulled off my flight to Baghdad to be sent to Afghanistan to get the investigation organized and ready for the general officer who would run the official inquiry. I was returning to Bagram just over three years after I left it.

After meeting with the deputy commander of CENTAF I was eventually brought into see Lt General North. I was always impressed by General North, a sharp leader and a fighter pilot with a long record of achievement. His job was to run two separate air wars; one in Iraq, and the other in Afghanistan while commanding tens of thousands of airmen, both US and coalition, across dozens of nations in Asia, Africa and the Middle East. But when I went in to see him for the first time, he was not a happy man. This friendly fire incident, which involved a close coalition ally, was just the sort of error that gets lots of bad press and weakens the coalition effort fighting the Taliban and Al Qaeda. I quickly learned that he was not a commander that you wanted to get on the wrong side of. He brought me to a variety of meetings regarding the incident. As I met various members of his staff, everyone pledged their support for me. Ironically, this was close to the same thing that happened when I was paraded through Prince Sultan Air Base (PSAB) in 2002 to meet the staff before I proceeded to Bagram (then considered the toughest air base in the world to run). Yet now North's staff was on the defensive, so it was not the same. After several hours of meetings, where I saw North at his most displeased, I was sent on my way to Afghanistan with this new task. I was proud that they had trusted me with such an important mission, but worried about how I was going to get it done properly.

I arrived in Afghanistan the next morning and went to what had been called Air Force Village, now named Camp Cunningham. The first thing I noticed was that the tents of my time had been replaced by wood buildings called 'B-huts' (long wood building that looked like chicken coops). My airmen had started the B-hut construction project in 2003, so it was nice to see them all completed. I was introduced to a few leaders and put into my own VIP B-hut. I immediately went to sleep as I had gone about three days without it. The next morning, I started the rounds - visiting the people who I needed to cajole into giving me a room, personnel and equipment for the investigation. I visited the commander of the 455th Expeditionary Wing at Bagram. There I was introduced to the new technology of the war front – video conferencing. It would play a critical role in my job at Sather AB, whenever I got there. This new technology fascinated me and would come to serve me well later in Iraq.

The next week went by quickly as I built a five-person team to sort the following information: cockpit HUD (heads up display or the video of what a pilot sees out the front of his aircraft) tapes, air traffic control audio tapes and initial reports from witnesses. We didn't analyze the data, we just got it ready for the general and his board of inquiry. I created a power point presentation on what he had organized and as a changeover tool for the general at the head of the board of inquiry.

Inquiry Board President Brigadier General (BG) Sid Clarke, and his deputy, Colonel John "Coach" Allison, came to Bagram after I had been there a week. They were both dedicated and smart individuals and graciously accepted the information and the presentation that I had built for them. As the changeover was occurring between BG Clarke and myself, General North also came to Bagram – this incident demanded that high level of command attention. He saw my briefing and then looked at the HUD tapes from the A-10 pilot who had accidently strafed the Canadian soldiers. The tape was damning because you could even see the shot which hit the vehicle where the Canadian soldiers had gathered.

The facts of the friendly fire incident painted a mixed picture of the event. The A-10 flight of two aircraft had been overhead and supporting the Canadians for over five hours. They stayed after their normal time on target had expired in order to keep hammering the Taliban fighters. Such a long flight is an extraordinary amount of time to be in combat and under pressure to hit the right targets.

The pilots were wearing night vision goggles (NVG), which are two small light amplifying tubes attached to the helmet that allow the pilots to see in complete darkness. They are amazing pieces of technology that give a green-tinted and almost 20/20 vision of the world outside the cockpit. But they do have their limitations, one of which bit this A-10 pilot. At the time of the incident, the morning sun was coming up in the sky. During this time (sunrise or sunset) a phenomenon in NVG flying called "changeover" occurs. The ground is still dark and you need to use the NVGs to see there, but the sky is becoming light which causes your eyes to begin to lose some of your night vision capability. At the same time, your NVGs begin to 'gain down' or reduce some of their sensitivity to light due to the sky lighting up. This changeover period means that the NVGs do not provide the same level of detail as before. Its' a subtle change as you enter into a region of reduced efficiency.

So, after five hours of flight, combat attacks and air refueling, all at night and under NVGs, the pilot hit the wrong target. He was told immediately of his error and the gravity hit him and his wingman like a freight train. I could tell from the tape that the pilot was deeply affected by this deadly mistake. What wasn't apparent on the tape was that the Canadian ground controller had given the tired pilot the wrong target to hit, a regrettable oversight but one that cost an Olympian his life. But that determination was in the future. I simply gave Lt Gen North and BG Clarke all the information and data for this inquiry. After over a week at Bagram I was on my way back to Iraq. I didn't know it, but this diversion would negatively affect my ability to prepare my people in the 447th AEG for their mission. All the personnel who arrived before I got to Iraq were briefed on the expectations for their tour by someone else. Not me. I'd have to find another way to give the airmen under my command my vision for their tour and what I expected from them.

I then travelled from Bagram to Balad AB, Iraq where I met the Iraqi air war commander, BG Robin Rand. I was surprised when he and his team met me as I got off the aircraft in Balad. After introductions, he took me to his office in Balad and gave me *his* expectations of me for my command in Iraq. I wrote down everything of significance on those items on which he briefed me.

His briefing to me was a shocker. I was expecting a pep talk or a list of expectations; what I got was a detailed program for presenting awards and decorations. When you observe a service member in their dress uniforms, you can see how many decorations they have received by how many ribbons are on their uniform. Generally, the longer one has been in the military or the more dangerous the job, the more decorations they will have received for achievement or heroism. Younger military members with a lot of ribbons usually means they received them for heroism in combat.

The level and amount of decorations has always been a problem for the Air Force in combat locations. The issue is not what the USAF awards to its personnel, but rather how much more generous the *U.S. Army* is with awards for its soldiers. When Air Force personnel talk to Army soldiers and see the disparity in the decorations they are receiving, jealousy sometimes develops.

The issue that Air Force personnel face is that the vast majority serve within the confines of a base; even if that base is subject to shelling, as happened during my deployment to Bagram AB, Afghanistan and Sather AB, Iraq. Air Force personnel also have the shortest tours in the AOR. The Army tours were for 1 year or more, Marines were there for 7 months and the Air Force tours were for 4-6 months (unless you were "extended" which happened to me in Afghanistan). Air Force folks also typically don't go "outside the wire", which means off-base, where bad things can happen and where most of the danger exists.

For the U.S. Air Force, most of those going outside the base into combat are the pilots and aircrew of the aircraft, the security forces, explosive ordnance disposal (EOD) and the Joint Terminal Attack Controllers (JTACs). In the Air Force, the officers generally do most of the fighting because they compromise the greatest percentage of combat aircrew. There are also Security Forces providing security for the bases or others assisting local police in the cities - such as the "in lieu of" Airmen we supported with the Chavis turret and vehicle maintenance. Another prominent group was explosive ordnance disposal (EOD), those that deal with the scourge of these latest conflicts, improvised explosive devices (IEDs) or home-made mines or bombs. The final combat airmen are the JTACs who accompany Army ground units by calling for and controlling air strikes. All these different groups in country represented only 1-5% of the USAF personnel in the AOR (CENTAF area of responsibility). Most airmen were not even based in a combat country and if they were, only a small percentage went outside the wire.

Yet to my mind, it was the "decoration inflation" practiced by the Army that hurt the other services. It's one thing to decorate those who served bravely in combat. It's another thing to hand out decorations to keep personnel in the service. People between the services observe, talk and desire the same for themselves. This had been a problem in Afghanistan and it was going to be a negative issue here in Iraq.

So, BG Rand and I were of one mind regarding decorations. Yet, he laid it out to me, in exacting detail (which I frantically wrote down in my small notebook), precisely how the decorations would be executed at Sather AB. Little did I realize that this conversation and my adherence to his desires would negatively affect my future promotion and career.

BG Rand wanted the Iraq campaign medal to be the main (and only) decoration for 80% of the Sather personnel. Those that would receive the Iraq campaign medal *and another one* had to be in leadership positions either as a senior NCO (non-commissioned officer) or as an officer and <u>done so successfully</u>. The larger your area of responsibility and the higher your rank, the greater was your decoration. He laid it out for me, by rank and decoration, as to who could receive what. For superstars, he would allow a couple people (out of 850 Air Force personnel in the 447th AEG) to move two decorations levels higher than the norm. These extraordinary personnel would need copious amounts of documentation for their accomplishments to receive these higher decorations. I already had a plan for our Sather decorations' program before this conversation, which I will detail later in this book. My plan was to celebrate everyone's Iraq campaign medal at the end of the tour.

By the time, I had written down everything from General Rand's 30-minute lecture on the Sather decorations program, I knew exactly how this agenda would go over when presented to the leadership at Sather – not very well. Still, it was something that had to be faced and BG Rand had made it clear that he was unhappy with my predecessor and his over-generous decorations program. He bluntly told me that if I repeated the same perceived errors as my forerunner, that his staff would reject my award's submissions. You want to reward your best people for their work in tough places like Sather AB and you don't want those high performers to leave the AOR with nothing to show for their superior achievement. I got the message loud and clear – follow these decoration guidelines and I'd get my requested decorations for my people.

After my initial meeting with BG Rand, I then had to spend the night at Balad before continuing on to BIAP and Sather AB. My torturous travel schedule to my deployment base was finally reaching its conclusion. I reached Sather the next day and my real adventure started immediately.

CHAPTER THREE
BUILDING AN INTRODUCTORY BRIEFING
TO INSTILL A WARRIOR MINDSET

My first goal after arriving at Sather was to go through the transition process of taking over command from my predecessor. In Afghanistan (2002, Bagram Air Base), I had to do that turnover of command in one insane, 18-hour day. Here at Sather, it was much more civilized. My predecessor was a genial Air Force Reserve (AFRC) wing commander from Dover Air Force Base, Delaware, and was a C-5 pilot. Sather Air Base was primarily a passenger and cargo transition point, in addition to providing air traffic control (ATC) services and base security forces. My predecessor's airlift background had given him an intuitive grasp of Sather's current operations. My experience was primarily in air-to-ground attack operations, so I had to expeditiously pick his brains on the basics of passenger and cargo handling.

My orientation covered not only Sather Air Base, but also the vast Victory Base Complex (VBC). I needed to get various ID access badges, get set into my quarters and learn how to find my way around VBC. I watched my predecessor give the introductory briefing to the new arrivals at Sather, a duty which would soon be mine. However, the two of us seemed to spend a great deal of our transition time visiting the nine other dining facilities or DFACs, generally referred to as "chow halls", run by civilian contractors on the Army bases. These visits largely concentrated on what entrée was served at which DFAC and on what day. At the time, I didn't understand his emphasis on where the best food was to be found on the various Army bases at VBC. The truth was that *Sather AB had no chow hall* and in order to eat you had to find a vehicle and drive to one of the other army compounds to do so. Within a few days of assuming command I would come to understand the huge number of man-hours wasted by this arrangement. For now, I was just slightly annoyed by the "quest for the best entrée" tour that I was receiving. I'd come to Sather to fight a war, not to keep myself happy with great meals all over VBC.

Within the next few days, I got acquainted with my staff and the change-of-command ceremony took place, with BG Rand there to say nice things about my predecessor before he departed for home. He had spent an extra 10 days waiting for me to arrive at Sather AB. Now I was in charge of Sather AB for the next four and a half months. Early in my tour BG (Brigadier General) Rand asked me to extend my tour for a couple extra weeks at Sather. I really had no good reason to refuse, so my tour was extended to help Rand smooth out the schedule for the changeover of his base commanders. That decision would later come back to haunt me.

The very first thing I began to do as commander was to re-write the commander's portion of the "Right Start" briefing. Why? Because I wanted to get my newly arriving airmen to think about being warriors, since we were in a conflict and their lives could conceivably be on the line. *I wanted them to feel the same passion that I felt toward winning this war.* I wanted them to develop a **WARRIOR ETHOS**. This had not been the normal path for most commanders at Sather AB previously. How did I know that? Because there was nothing about it in the previous briefing. In the USAF, the "Right Start" program was the long introductory briefing for all airmen at a new base. For a combat base like Sather this briefing was pretty comprehensive. By adding my portion, I aimed to make it better.

The Right Start briefing, and especially the commander's portion of that, was about getting everyone 'on the same page' about what life would be like during their tour. The USAF had a unique way to accomplish their combat deployments. Unlike the Army or the Marines, where they were members from a single unit that had worked or trained before, the Air Force brought people in from all over the world thrown together haphazardly.

In the late '90's, the USAF instituted the Air Expeditionary Force (AEF) system to provide a level of predictability to unit deployments. The 447th AEG (Air Expeditionary Group) had 850 mixed USAF, Air Force Reserve (AFR) and Air National Guard (ANG) personnel from over 60 bases across the globe. Few had trained together before. It was a "plug and play" system that had been in existence since Operation DESERT STORM in 1990. If you needed a typist for a tour the first option was to get a volunteer from throughout the Air Force Reserve or Air National Guard. If the position couldn't be filled from those organizations, then a person was assigned to it from the USAF active duty ranks. Individuals were chosen by the unit commander from a wing. AEF tours were usually 120-180 days in length.

You would think that personnel for combat deployments would be chosen for their merit or experience. Yet unfortunately, some commanders used it to send us their "problem children", substandard or low performers. Or even brand-new personnel right out of their job school. Personnel that could be dumped at a far-away place for 4-6 months. The plug and play system thus meant that there was a wide variety of talent and motivation for the airmen at Sather AB. I needed these people to get immediately into a combat mindset.

Why develop a Warrior Mentality for my airmen? Because there was a real enemy that presented an asymmetric threat, using unconventional tactics. I knew those with a warrior fierceness would give it their all. Because warriors don't complain. Because a warrior will do whatever it takes to help us win this war. Although the USAF tours were the shortest of any service, they were the most work oriented. There were two shifts – day and night. Everyone worked a minimum of 12 hours a day, every day. No days off - no holidays. There was a minimum of personnel. For instance, we were moving cargo from USAF aircraft at a rate equivalent to a large Air Force base with *ten times* our number of people! That's what 'combatant thinking' gets you. I needed a maximum effort for our tour and I wanted my airmen to think like warriors. This was not a cheap slogan but a real mindset for people that weren't used to being fighters.

My briefing to my Airmen stated that I had four main objectives for the 447th AEG and for them at Sather Air Base (AB).

- Accomplish the mission
- Bring you home alive
- Leave this base better
- Make you better

"Accomplish the mission" meant doing their job at the maximum level for the tour. Every single person has a part to play in winning a war. Every role is important. Sather's small part in the Iraq War was to move Soldiers, Marines and cargo safely from the big Air Force cargo planes (such as the C-17, C-130 and C-5) onto the Army helicopters that took them to their FOBs (Forward Operating Bases). For the Airmen working every single day for 4-6 months this may seem like an easy task. But it quickly became a grind. There was no leave, no booze or no days off. Creating a warrior mindset and making everyone feel that they have an important job to play was the leadership objective – my objective.

"Bringing you home alive" was about security in a dangerous place. Although not apparent to our leadership at Balad, we were getting shelled from Baghdad (see Chapter 6) every few days. I knew that because I was being called often with reports like, "we saw an explosion north in the junkyard" (rocket attack), or "there was a big splash in the sand near the runway, but no explosion" (dud enemy ordnance), etc. There were other dangers for our people, especially women, at the other Army & contractor bases in VBC. I told my Airmen that if they followed my guidelines, participated in the training I set up, that I would do everything in my power to get them home alive. For instance, Sather AB during my tour, was the *only* base in our time in Iraq (or Afghanistan) to hold special warrior training and practice readiness exercises based on my commands (Chapter 6). I would make sure everyone was ready for our time in Iraq, no matter what the enemy threw at us.

"Make this place better" is the obvious improvement of any base during your time there. I arrived ready to solve problems, although initially I thought that there would be few, if any, issues for me to handle. Besides working 12-hours per day, I also asked my people to give another hour (per day) toward making the camp a better place to live. I wanted work toward voluntary projects, for morale purposes. At Bagram AB, Afghanistan we used this excess energy to help build a movie tent, increase the size of the camp gymnasium and for a weekly steak night, to name a few examples. At Sather, this emphasis was on morale boosting events and ideas. My contributions at Sather Air Base were the concept for "State Street", the Sandlot Football League, as well as "Cheyenne's Grill". The idea was that our people would come up with morale concepts of their own to make Sather better during this tour. If everyone dedicated themselves to these projects, the base would improve quickly. Leadership must always encourage and be responsive to any ideas that improve morale.

Finally, the last theme of this tour was to "Make You Better". This was a 4-6-month period away from family, friends and the normal lifetime distractions. I strongly encouraged airmen to try to improve themselves. Instead of worrying about what one didn't have (like alcohol), it was time to try to use that as an advantage toward personal progress. Many took advantage of this period to take the classes that we helped to organize such as "Weight Loss", "Quit Smoking", "Pass the PFT (Physical Fitness Test)", etc. We also added mandatory classes on combat first aid (in the USAF, its' called Self Aid and Buddy Care - SABC), a required run/walk for 1.5 miles in body armor (about 65 pounds) and four separate readiness exercises centered around simulated enemy rocket attacks. The point is: if you give people activities to improve themselves, many will do so. *It's better for people to participate in positive activities than for them to invent negative ones.* I wanted future camp activities to be centered around the upbeat themes that I began in my commander's presentation.

Another section that I added to the commander's briefing had to do with unit history. When new units were created in the desert, for this Iraq War, the Air Force picked unit numbers from the most storied squadrons, groups and wings from prior conflicts. For instance, the 332nd Wing, which was our headquarters unit in Balad Air Base, was a historical unit from WWII. It was the fabled "Tuskegee Airmen" – a famous black fighter unit in the European Theater.

Using the internet, I researched our historical unit from World War II (WWII), the 447th Bomber Group (BG). It had its own website complete with multitudes of combat pictures! Our historical group also had a bloodied and courageous story. Therefore, I took the 447th BG's WWII history and told it to our airmen. Once again, this was about getting our people to think and act like warriors.

The 447th had been a B-17 "Flying Fortress" bomber unit that had fought over Europe in WWII from early in the war until its end. Many of its airmen were killed in action, wounded or became prisoners of war (POWs). Whenever our current people thought that they had it tough or felt sorry for themselves I wanted them to remember the photographs of shot up B-17's, the wounded or killed airmen, or those who spent years in a German POW camp. *Those people* had it tough compared to our current situation!

Using our unit's storied history to "toughen up" our people had worked. The historical approach to toughen up our people was a great idea. However, it only added about 5-10 minutes to the overall briefing. There were some great B-17 aircraft pictures, considering the level of camera technology back in the 1940's. These pictures were not of a pristine B-17 in a museum but of the actual aircraft that had crash-landed, been hit by anti-aircraft fire or strafed by German fighter aircraft.

Other ideas I incorporated into the Right Start briefing were unique issues about our base at Sather. We had no crime at Sather even though everyone lived in "open bay" tents (eight people per tent) with unguarded lockers (no locks on them). Conversely the Army and contractor's camps in VBC were suffering crime on a large scale. It didn't happen to us because we had a sense of community at our base. I wanted our people to feel and keep that sense of pride and community. So, I talked about our "safe neighborhood" and how we were going to keep that.

Sather was the only camp that was closed to outsiders. You could only enter with a special ID card - whereas the other VBC camps were open to everyone. People in VBC lived in trailers with locked doors and had lock-bolted storage boxes. There was still thievery and assaults on personnel in VBC. My briefing talked about the safety of Sather, versus the crime in VBC. Our people wanted Sather to be safe and it worked. My briefing hit that point again and again and made it a reality.

Early in the tour, I offered combat first aid training to the civilian workers at Sather. The biggest citizen group was a band of women who worked in our small exchange shop (similar to a mini-market). They were frightened by the constant gunfire at night from a nearby Iraqi Special Operations Camp and the occasional shelling. I said to them, "Get the training that all of the USAF people have and you won't be afraid". They took the training and my Right Start briefing in October and thus became part of the Sather team. They even started to sell "Sather AB" hats and t-shirts in their store based on my urging.

My final coup was to get all of the Army personnel who worked on Sather, but didn't live there, to receive our Right Start program. I did it in exchange for allowing Army vehicle repair work in our USAF maintenance building. Thus, I was able to "spread the word" to all the personnel of Sather, not just the Air Force people. It brought everyone closer, built a sense of community and raised the training level for everyone on the base. From that point on every service participated in our base-wide training exercises. This was the only time at Sather, before or since, where all the services, including civilians, participated in our base-wide readiness exercises.

As time went on I added our group's many accomplishments to the Right Start briefing. I also did not shy away from talking about our problem areas. Of particular importance in the Right Start briefing was a definitive slide on the General Order One Alpha (GO1A) program. The GO1A dealt with some of the 'Vietnam legacy' issues. These are the areas **prohibited** by GO1A:

- Alcohol
- Pornography
- Personal Firearms or Explosives
- Gambling
- Opposite Sex Visitation
- Detainee or Human Remains Photos

The message on what was prohibited was followed by a very stern warning on how violations were going to be addressed. First, all violations of GO1A were going to be prosecuted immediately, with no exceptions of any kind. Secondly, they would most likely be addressed, in country, by an Article 15 - non-judicial punishment. An Article 15 is serious business, an action below the level of a courts martial levied by an individual's unit commander. Finally, the Article 15 punishment would be served out *in theater*. Punishment would happen at one's combat location versus being sent home. For example, one of my security forces airmen lost all of her rank, due to a GO1A violation, which means she surrendered all of her stripes while at Sather AB. In summary, the Right Start commander's briefing helped me to present what I wanted our personnel to become – that is warriors on the mission of their lives.

The expansion of the Commander's portion of the Right Start briefing was one critical part of developing the Warrior Ethos for all the members that received it. Unfortunately, because of my detour to Afghanistan, I was not able to give my speech to everyone in the 447th AEG during our tour (ironically, I was able to brief everyone in the next deployment, due to the extension of my tour). I needed another way to get the word out to those who didn't get my "warrior creed" message. My solution to this issue was to conduct a base inspection very early in my tour.

CHAPTER FOUR
BASE INSPECTION

I knew from the start of my tour that many of my personnel and officers had not seen or heard my commander's briefing and might not understand my priorities. Therefore, I felt it was extremely important for me to introduce myself to my airmen as well as to familiarize myself with the issues and problems of Sather AB. Having been a wing commander, I felt the best way to accomplish these two tasks was to conduct a base-wide inspection. That way I could meet most of the airmen at Sather and become acquainted with all the functional areas on the base. So, during my very first staff meeting I briefed the Sather leadership that I would be personally walking throughout the camp. That would entail the inspection of every building and room at Sather Air Base.

The base inspection is important because the commander is the only one who can tie together all the aspects of base. It's one thing to drive around a base and to become somewhat familiar with the base structure. It's another to really know every facet of the air base in a short amount of time. Because of the relatively short duration of the Air Force tours, usually 4-6 months, there was a great *lack of long-term continuity* due to this constant turnover. I received a good handoff from my predecessor, yet I knew little of what happened a year or more ago before at Sather. Without doing a base-wide inspection many items would slide into the cracks, for example, finding simple things like keys to locks and doors that had been lost over time. By doing a base inspection not only did I know everything about the base, but I also made sure each officer and senior NCO was familiar with *their* area of responsibility also.

I told each area commander that this inspection would not be a "white glove" assessment. But, this was not exactly true, because the best leaders would clean up their areas before I arrived. I was not interested in an immaculate, sanitized building, but rather an organized and spruced up one. It is better to start a tour with an orderly and logical tidying then to continue with the apathy that can creep over time.

As I said in the Right Start commander's briefing, the "cruising through the tour" mentality was not how I was going to run the 447th AEG. By conducting a commander's inspection, I intended to show everyone that we were going to run a tight ship during this tour. I had four purposes to this inspection:

- Introduce myself to the Airmen

- Have the Airmen introduce themselves to me and tell me their jobs at Sather

- Clean up and organize individual areas

- Identify problems in individual sections or issues that were base-wide

I began my base inspection within my first week of assuming command at Sather. Attending me was my Second-in-Command, LtCol (Lieutenant Colonel) Preston Smith; my Senior NCO, CMSgt (Chief Master Sergeant) Gordon Swarthout, a representative from the civil engineering squadron and the officers-in-charge of all areas that we would be inspecting, along with his or her senior NCO. Notes would be taken of problem areas from every section.

In the very first section, we came upon locked doors to rooms and to a 'Conex' (a 20 or 40' intermodal container for shipping or storage). I had stated at the staff meeting that we would wait for a key to be found for the door or conex locks. Sure enough, we ended up pausing our inspection until keys or bolt cutters could be found. After the word got around about the embarrassment of standing around until access was gained, the problem disappeared.

Almost immediately a Sather-wide problem became evident, which wouldn't have been discovered without this inspection. About a third of the individual Conex's (shipping containers) showed signs of water and mud damage from flooding prior to my arrival and had affected some sections of the base. Many of these Conexes were just sitting on the ground which made them vulnerable to water damage, even though we were in a desert area. Most of the contents within these particular containers had been destroyed or damaged by the flooding. This long-term problem would have gone undiscovered had we not conducted this inspection. We prevented further Conex flooding for years to come by raising up any that showed past water damage. We also had ditches dug to help drain problem areas. The failure to fix this serious problem over the previous three and a half years was an indication that this issue was one that had slipped through the cracks due to the continual commander changeovers.

All that had been done about the flooding in the past was to simply remove the water-logged parts and equipment from the Conex's *without correcting* the underlying drainage problem. Over the following year, the individual Conex's were slowly filled with new material, which would be subject to destruction during the next winter rains. This was an example of a waste of resources, despite a remarkably easy fix of raising up the Conexes on wood rails.

The next problem area that we encountered was what I call the "bucket of keys". Most doors throughout the base had locks on them. All the Conexes had padlocks of all shapes and sizes. From tour to tour the keys for these locks were misplaced or lost. Only by doing a thorough examination of the base were we able to get a handle on the key and lock situation. As I said, from the first embarrassing situations where we sat around trying to get the right key for a lock or door, the buckets of keys quickly sorted themselves out as we changed locks and door handles until we ascertained which keys went where.

The final area where this inspection made a huge impact was in the supply arena. The logistics unit had a very large Quonset hut that had been packed haphazardly with office and equipment supplies in a completely disorganized manner. There was no computerized list of any of the contents, so people just kept ordering and reordering office and supply material until they finally left for home, when the reorder loop would continue with the next group. The result was a massive building filled with stocks and stores of material whose contents were unknown and for which there was no accountability. Our energetic Logistics Group commander, LtCol (Lieutenant Colonel) Mike Cannon, had his people spend over a week going through this Quonset hut, in an arduous effort to straighten out this horrible mess. They found literally *hundreds of thousands of dollars* of unused office supplies and equipment. They gathered it, categorized what we needed and sent the rest back to the U.S. – saving all of that money for the war effort. They completely cleaned up the big hut and then built a computerized list of equipment that was now stored at Sather. LtCol Cannon's people were justifiably proud of the work that they had done and were very happy to show it to me. I was also excited to see the great progress that they had made on the Quonset hut and the vast amount of supplies that were saved.

As I toured the newly organized storage building, they asked me if I needed anything. I said that I needed a stapler. They gave me a big, battery powered stapler that could probably clip together a dictionary! I decided as a joke to create my own urban legend with the stapler by calling it "Saddam's Power Stapler". I had one of the translators write in Arabic, using permeant ink on the stapler, "Supreme Leader of Iraq". From then on as a practical joke, I told everyone of the stapler's supposed origin.

As the inspection wound the way through the camp I saw everything from a derelict anti-aircraft gun to Saddam Hussein's favorite blue farm tractor. Near the end of my tour I found serious security problems in the EOD (Explosive Ordnance Disposal) and Fire Departments quarters. I also found even more severe security issues with the Baghdad International Airport (BIAP) control tower. All these issues would be addressed over time, but none were known to me before the base inspection. Only by visually looking at the base's problems in the micro and macro level could major problem areas be recognized and resolved.

It took me about three weeks to move throughout the base on this tour, hitting different sections on separate days. It took another two months to finally correct all of the drainage and security issues brought up by the inspection. But the good news was that problems were getting fixed, which had gone unaddressed for *years*! The other byproducts of the inspection can't be over-stated. Sections were cleaned up and organized right at the beginning of the tour, which helped make the deployment go more smoothly. I was able to meet in person many of the airmen whom I hadn't been able to brief.

The base inspection really was a great starting point for many of the biggest projects that the 447th AEG handled during our tour. Only by seeing the problems in total were they easily discernible to myself and the staff. None of the major undertakings would have happened without the inspection to highlight them.

CHAPTER FIVE
FEEDING THE HUNGRY

This is a story of how listening to one small voice can result in a huge morale improvement for an entire base. In this case, hearing one persons' problem brought a serious issue to light, and by doing so it was addressed to the benefit of the entire Group.

This tale started during the command changeover with my predecessor, when I was introduced to all nine of the Army dining halls (DFACs) scattered throughout the Victory Base Complex. Each of these dining halls had been organized by the Army, however, the actual cooking and food preparation was done by a civilian company. I had seen this before; when I was in Afghanistan, the chow halls had been switched over from Army cooks to civilian contractors, which resulted in a great improvement in the quality of the food. Still, the issue was that Sather Air Base had no chow hall of its own.

In Iraq, the food was generally outstanding, in terms of variety and quality, at the Army bases. Yet the issue at Sather AB was, in order to get *one meal*, you had to have access to a vehicle, which not everyone had, plus it required 1 and a half hours to travel to another Army camp over poor roads, process through the various checkpoints, find parking and then stand in line. I timed it on one breakfast meal just to see how much time I wasted to eat. Multiply that by three meals a day and we discovered it took almost 5 hours out of every workday, just to eat! Because of my frantic work schedule, I didn't have the five hours to spend going to DFACs at other bases. As a result, I missed a lot of meals at the beginning of my tour.

Several of the bigger squadrons, such as the Security Forces, which had over 100 personnel, had set up their own mini-dining tents. However, these could only be used by the members of that unit. I have to say that going without many meals in the beginning really made me grouchy, which was felt by my staff. Still, I did not appreciate the real impact of this issue on the 447th AEG, until about a week into my tour.

One of the very good practices carried over from the active duty USAF was a meeting set up between the commander and about two dozen young airmen, termed the "Rising Six", which occurred very early in the tour. The Rising Six was a cross section of the <u>lowest</u> ranking personnel from the different units in the 447th. This meant that I was meeting with sharp personnel from the 18-24 years old group. During my first meeting with the Rising Six I talked about my philosophy for our tour and the fact that good ideas can come from anyone with the courage to espouse them. Although most good notions would eventually be relayed up the rank structure, the Rising Six meeting allowed the younger troops to talk to me directly.

After waxing on about my desire for a Warrior Ethos including having my core concepts of "Fulfilling the mission", "Bringing everyone home", "Making the base and each deployed airman better", I asked the Rising Six for their feedback, noting that, "this was the time to tell me directly of *any* problems that they were experiencing at Sather". There was a pause. No one wanted to be the first to speak. Finally, an 18-year old Airman named Cheyenne Kutak bravely raised her hand and said that she worked on the night shift in the base Post Office. She stated that, because of her nighttime schedule, *she often went hungry.* Her comment immediately struck a chord with me about the food issue at Sather, since I was experiencing the same issue myself. Sather Air Base had no dining hall. Getting meals was a problem even if you had a vehicle (which many did not have). I immediately asked the other members of the Rising Six: "how many of them usually went without at least one meal a day?" I was shocked when *every single young person* raised their hand! The question that I wished I had asked later was how many Airmen normally went without two meals a day? I immediately understood that only the officers and senior enlisted had access to vehicles to go eat at the neighboring Army dining halls. The youngest members of the 447th, unless they belonged to one of the bigger squadrons with their own chow tent, were going hungry. *In fact, I recognized that the younger someone was at Sather, the less chance that they had getting fed.*

Why didn't Sather distribute packaged Meals Ready to Eat (MRE's) to those who did not have access to a vehicle? Because for three and a half years no one in a leadership position had determined that the lowest ranks weren't getting fed. I consider this to be a failure on the part of the USAF leadership to ensure their deployed airmen had their basic needs met.

Besides doing the mission, it is the primary job of a commander to make sure the troops are fed and have a place to sleep. I was puzzled that no one had done something about this issue before. This would not be the first time I asked this question during my tour. I talked with the Rising Six further about this food issue and immediately made the following statement: "We will have a Sather dining tent with basic food service within one week from this meeting". I said the same thing at my weekly staff meeting. I didn't know all the issues necessary to get a dining tent running, but one week seemed reasonable to me. This statement drove the project. Resolving this problem would greatly raise morale and productivity for the entire camp. Furthermore, this was exactly the sort of feedback that we needed from people to fix the issues at the base.

Several things became apparent once we began to look into the food issue at Sather. First of all, there was a USAF long-term plan to get food at the base with the construction of a Sather DFAC building, due in the November-December 2006-time frame. Secondly, the USAF had been assigning a *couple dozen* Airmen per tour to count the number of military persons eating at each Army DFAC. I termed these personnel as the "clicker airmen" because they used a simple counting machine to keep track of the people entering a dining hall. The cooking companies were paid by the number of meals provided, thus these clicker airmen were the "tax" that Army was charging the Air Force for using their dining halls. So, every 4-6 months, a couple dozen airmen were being sent to Iraq whose sole purpose was to count people coming into the Army dining tents. I put an end to that job and the "tax" as soon as we had our own dining tent, making those airmen really happy to get back to the normal Air Force mission at Sather.

Establishing a new chow hall on-base at Sather certainly created excitement. There was a buzz in the camp about this project. However, I got immediate pushback from an unexpected source. The First Lieutenant (1Lt) in charge of the Services squadron, the unit which would be arranging for the food service, gave me the initial feedback that, "this will be difficult to organize and execute in one week". I was really surprised by this comment, although as time went on, I recognized that he lacked the initiative for handling difficult issues. Still, I made it clear that this was a huge problem at Sather, impacting the junior enlisted personnel and that I expected it to be completed in a week, as I had promised.

We quickly located an empty tent and tables for the dining hall that would be was centrally located and within walking distance for everyone on Sather. The biggest obstacle was negotiating with the Army to supply food in plastic tubs. Our initial goal was to have them supply B- or T-rations, precooked meals that could be immersed in hot water to warm them. We were only going to provide 5-6 different servings, which was far less variety than what was offered in the normal Army DFACs, but they were better than the MREs, and would be accessible to everyone on the base. I decided to call the dining tent "Cheyenne's Grill" after the very young airman who first raised the issue of the food service problem at Sather. We also decided that there would be a fitness competition from all the 447th squadrons, with a man and woman from each unit doing pushups and sit ups to determine which unit would enter the dining tent first on opening day.

Six days after the Rising Six meeting, I asked how the preparations for the opening day of the chow tent were coming. Once again, I got an extremely lukewarm answer from the Services Commander, to the effect that we might have it ready in a week or two. I didn't exactly explode but very emphatically told my deputy commander, LtCol Smith and senior NCO, CMSgt Swarthout, that I had promised this in a week and it would be done on schedule. I gave them full authority and tasking to take over the preparations from the lackadaisical Services unit. Smith and Swarthout immediately took the reins and ran with the project, negotiating with the Army for everything we wanted. The Army would stop supplying all the bigger squadrons at Sather who had their own meal programs and consolidate all the food service at Cheyenne's Grill. As for getting back our 2-3 dozen airmen "clickers" the Army simply said, "We were wondering when you USAF guys would stop supplying them to us". This was the sort of project that LtCol Smith was good at – a single assignment with a clear and immediate objective. He and

CMSgt Swarthout made it all work in a single day.

The promised opening day dawned clear and blue, as usual, and the first meal to be served was lunch. All the big 447th units supplied their best man and woman for the physical fitness contest. Before the competition started I gave a vigorous pep talk about how courageous Airman Cheyenne Kutak had been to highlight this issue. The problem was raised and fixed in one week, as promised.

We had Airman Kutak pull off a camouflage netting and a large wood plague that said "Cheyenne's Grill" underneath. The fitness test enthusiastically went off as advertised and I even participated in it. The two contest winners rang a large cow bell outside the dining tent and the winning unit lined up to be the first to eat. We all then lined up to eat at Sather AB for the first time in three and a half years. Cheyenne's Grill was a massive morale boost for the base. It was a place where all ranks ate together and we even had televisions hooked up to show the Armed Forces TV Network. The food tent served the base from late September until Christmas Eve and provided over 75,000 meals. Although the variety of servings was very limited, it was a big improvement over the previous arrangement and resolved the difficulty in obtaining meals for most of the enlisted personnel. Of all the morale events and activities that we did during our tour at Sather, the opening of the food tent was by far the most popular. Spirits rose appreciably when we opened this tent, for me and everyone else. That, and the fact that we saved literally tens of thousands of hours of work hours for the 447th by not having to drive to other bases to eat. It was a victory for the base.

As for the upcoming Air Force DFAC we had some fun with that also. The Civil Engineering Commander made a bold prediction in October that the DFAC would be ready by Thanksgiving Day (Nov 25th, 2006). When that day came, and went, with the DFAC being far from ready, all the other commanders and I had a humorous photo taken, showing our feigned disappointment. We showed this picture at our next staff meeting to much laughter.

The actual dedication of the DFAC was held on Christmas night in 2006. The commander of CENTAF, LtGen North came in for the dedication. As I said in the Chavis turret story, North was briefed by me on all of the accomplishments of the 447th AEG during our tour on this visit. He also participated in a ceremony where we presented Iraq campaign medals to 20 personnel. Therefore, it was a really upbeat holiday. On Christmas night, we went over to the DFAC building for the ceremony.

I gave a short but fiery speech about how I had named the chow hall. It is in the tradition of the Air Force to name bases after fallen and heroic Airmen. We determined to name the dining hall the "Technical Sergeant (TSgt) Walter M. Moss, Jr. Airpower DFAC". TSgt Moss was a learned and well-respected member of the EOD (Explosive Ordnance Disposal) team who was killed in action in March, 2006. This dining hall building was given his name to honor his sacrifice.

I also said in my speech that we called it an "Airpower" DFAC because that was the mission of the Air Force: to provide air power for the soldiers, marines and even airmen fighting on the ground in Iraq. The U.S. Air Force didn't name our only DFAC (unlike those of the Army in VBC), "Oasis", "DeFluery", "International Café" or even "DFAC #1". We named it after a man and our mission in Iraq. Furthermore, I made sure that we covered the walls of the DFAC with pictures of the people of the 447th AEG and the aircraft in the Air Force over the last 90 years. I even picked out four pictures of the A-10 as well as a description of the aircraft for use in the DFAC.

I wanted to make sure the history of the Air Force was reflected on the walls of DFAC for all the visitors to see. Finally, after LtGen North spoke, the two of us pulled off a camouflaged banner covering the name of the DFAC. We then sang the Air Force song to end the night. Sather Air Base now had its own real chow hall. We'd come a long way from our little Cheyenne's Grill, but that one project had raised morale, increased productivity by not forcing deployed airmen to either have to drive to other bases to eat or else go hungry. It also saved several dozen airmen from doing a ridiculous and nonproductive job as a "clicker". It took the courage of a very young airman to tell us of a big problem at Sather Air Base and we made it right in short order.

CHAPTER SIX
SECURITY BLACK HOLES AND BASE OPERATIONAL READINESS EXERCISES (OREs)
"Eye of the Hurricane"

Looking at Sather Air Base, you would think that it would be a relatively safe place to work, despite being just miles from the tough streets of Baghdad. It was located in the middle of the large Victory Base Complex with roughly 60,000 Army soldiers populating the bases in this area. VBC was protected by the new C-RAM (Counter Rocket, Artillery, Mortar) system which gave very loud verbal warnings ("Incoming, Incoming"), broadcast by large speakers throughout VBC, when rockets were coming toward the base. Much of Sather Air Base was surrounded by high concrete walls. We had over 100 Air Force Security Force personnel patrolling the base area on a 24/7 basis. However, looks were very deceiving.

First of all, during our time period, the C-RAM did not seem to work well. Through my entire tour, we did not receive a single warning of a rocket attack, even when a 107 mm Russian rocket exploded 30 yards from a C-5 Galaxy aircraft on the Sather aircraft ramp, when I personally saw several rockets blast through the BIAP passenger terminal roof or when one blew up 800 yards away from us on the Iraqi air base on New Al Muthana. The one time we actually got the jarring warning from C-RAM, nothing happened, so it was either a false alarm or else the incoming round was a dud.

During my Commander's changeover in September 2006, I asked my predecessor if the 447th AEG had done any sort of training during his tenure as commander. He said that, "We don't do training in wartime". This would not be my philosophy during our tour in Iraq. We would practice and prepare for any contingency that I considered likely to happen during our time at Sather Air Base.

Our most serious threat at Sather Air Base were the random rockets that impacted the base. I told our Airmen that this was the "Eye of the Hurricane". We were the "eye" surrounded by Baghdad and its environs, which could be used by the militias for rocket firing positions. The great concern was that everyone on Sather lived in tents, which provided little protection from rocket shrapnel. Sather Air Base fell under the umbrella of the VBC Counter Rocket, Artillery, Mortar (C-RAM) system, which was supposed to detect incoming projectiles. The systems radar would detect the rounds, activate an alarm system via giant speakers throughout the base, then engage the round(s) with a 20 mm Gatling gun. I had actually seen the C-RAM system work beautifully at Balad Air Base by successfully warning us of the attack and engaging the mortar rounds. However, during my tenure at Sather, the alarms only activated once and that one was either a dud or a false alarm. Yet, I kept getting calls, every few days, from the air traffic control tower and other observation points on our base reporting loud explosions, radar plots, the flash of a rocket detonating on the Sather property or else large plumes of dust when the rocket was a dud (failed to detonate).

The numerous rocket attacks against Sather AB manifested themselves in various ways. The better aimed, functioning rockets produced a loud explosion and rain of fragments. Poorly aimed rockets detonated in the empty portions of the base and far enough away that there was only the flash of the detonation but no sound. Often, all we heard was just a boom. Once in a while, we received the word of a radar plot of a rocket hit with or without the explosion or sound. There were times when we would only observe a large plume of dust at the impact point, meaning the rocket was a dud. How did we know that these were rocket attacks and not mortars or artillery? The range from Baghdad was too far for mortars and the anti-government forces did not have any artillery. Typically, I'd get notification of a rocket attack at 2:00 am via a phone call to my quarters informing me that the control tower had seen a large explosion in the aircraft junk yard. Since most of Sather was open desert these explosions usually caused no damage. Also, many of the calls were generated when a dust plume was observed somewhere. I recall one that impacted right next to a departing C-130 Hercules aircraft as it taxied out for takeoff. The aircraft pilot reported a large dust plume off to one side of the aircraft with no explosion. We surmised that it was a dud munition. The C-130 took off without incident, but it showed that the enemy had the range of our airfield and that the mega-expensive C-RAM system was not effectively covering us at Sather Air Base.

I questioned a civilian contractor who helped operate the C-RAM system at VBC on our lack of warning or engagements. He and I surmised that the rockets may have been fired at such a low trajectory that they were, literally, flying under the radar coverage. Years later, I found some videos showing the less sophisticated militias piling small mounds of dirt, leaning the rockets against them, pointed in the general direction of the target, then lighting a fabricated fuse and fleeing. This type of operation explained the random nature of the attacks, as well as the lack of engagements by C-RAM.

The problem generated by the lack of the C-RAM alarms was that, as far as the leadership at Balad and Al Udeid was concerned, Sather Air Base did not have a rocket problem. Since we had no C-RAM warnings, by that measure we had experienced no rocket attacks. I would have been justified in doing little or nothing concerning the rocket attacks, as all my predecessors had done. Yet, the calls I received from the command post of rockets hitting across the base told a different story and I felt strongly that my staff must vigorously respond to the rocket problem.

I do not know of how many rockets hit Sather during my tenure. Yet, as I said, I kept receiving phone calls throughout the tour of rocket attack evidence (explosions, flashes, booms, radar plots and large dust plumes) every few days. In retrospect, I should have kept track of the rocket attacks from the beginning. Belatedly, I did try to have my command post record each rocket attacks at the end of the tour. However, I was initially *shocked* at the number of rocket events and the fact that we were so ill-prepared for them. I was far more concerned with our response to this real threat, via our planned training, exercises, building of bomb shelters and blast barriers than with establishing this metric that I could not prove, without the C-RAM alarms.

When I reported the rocket attack that "moderately" damaged a C-5 aircraft on our ramp in December, 2006 via my daily secret Situation Report (SITREP), and stated that we had received no C-RAM warning, nor 20 mm gun engagement, I got no response from headquarters. We were on our own to deal with the rocket threat at Sather.

Another security problem had to do with Baghdad International Airport (BIAP). We were butted right against the airport with some of our positions only 300 yards from the civilian side there. Forty percent of Sather Air Base was surrounded by high concrete walls but the rest faced civilian-controlled BIAP where there were no barriers or even a fence. Some of our US Air Force personnel worked with Iraqi civilians in the BIAP control tower and they had no identification badges or nametags of any kind. Nor did these civilian workers have to go through any security checkpoint to get to the tower.

Very early in my tour I went on a visit over to BIAP with a concerned State Department official. Once, the airport was a well-constructed and maintained site, built to European standards. Now many of the buildings, especially those closest to Sather AB, were completely derelict and vacant. Breaking a couple locks into these BIAP structures would gain one access to these forlorn buildings and give a straight line-of-sight access to point guns, rockets or mortars to Sather Air Base at close range. Could enemy agents be using these supposedly empty buildings to watch or target Sather Air Base?

The only airport defense on BIAP was a British-owned security company that had never been paid by the Iraqi government. You would think a European security company would be top-notch and squared away. It wasn't. The head security manager was a well-spoken, urbane British national. The next level of company managers under him were English-speaking expatriates. However, once one went down the organizational chart for this security company, you met the worker bees - who all were Muslim workers from places such a Bangladesh, Malaya and Indonesia. These employees were well intentioned but provided no real security against a well-trained and motivated enemy. When we went through checkpoints in BIAP we often brought food for these poor fellows.

At several of the checkpoints between BIAP and Sather AB there were small shacks built for these security workers to use as guard posts. However, every night, these security personnel would build a fire to keep warm and then promptly fall asleep for the night. I know this because I went on patrols with our Security Forces on Sather and we would approach these checkpoints while wearing night vision goggles (NVGs), sometimes to less than 5 yards away from them. Yet the sleeping guards never knew of our presence scouting out their positions. Not only was the BIAP security weak, but we never knew if the British security company would simply pack their bags and leave because of non-payment. We considered the BIAP security force, unreliable as it was, to be at risk of disappearing at any time and had a contingency plan to replace them if they left.

Other problems quietly but quickly became evident during my initial tour of BIAP. As we patrolled BIAP with the U.S. State Department representative, I was taken to see an enormous, non-functioning generator. The Iraqis were hoping that I could help them get the generator fixed. What I saw on my generator tour was far more alarming than just an out-of-service machine. While inspecting the generator building, we passed through the worker's locker room. On some of the lockers were stickers for Jaysh Al-Mahdi (JAM), a violent anti-government group! I was shocked to see these so brazenly exhibited. I even went back to the lockers by myself to take photos of those with the decals. It was as if you went to any workplace in America where people had work lockers and saw a bunch of Communist symbols on them. This made me wonder how many workers at the airport were silent supporters of the anti-government groups in Iraq?

As if I wasn't alarmed enough during my tour of BIAP, I next visited a part of the airfield where there were empty storage buildings. Suddenly, our group began being followed by a group of Iraqis who were not part of the BIAP security company and were obviously not happy to see us there. The guards we brought with us on this visit became very nervous at the Iraqi attention and armed their weapons.

The reason for the excessive attention we received from Iraqis around these empty BIAP storage buildings became obvious to me later in my tour. By October, 2006 I began to see internal Office of Special Investigation (OSI) reports on the dangerous activities of the anti-government forces in BIAP. They were moving Iranian-supplied weapons and money into Iraq via commercial aircraft. These storage building were probably the location where this dangerous booty was being placed. We just happened to stumble upon these storage areas when they were empty. If we had walked into them when they were being used, we probably would have been in for a gun battle!

After seeing the empty buildings with all that nefarious attention from unknown Iraqis, we found a separate guarded munitions storage area. This ammunition space was surrounded by a fence, but was anything but secure. First of all, there were holes in the fence. The four armed guards took us into the munitions area and let us walk around. We found large stacks of new, boxed AK-47 rifles, ammunitions and grenades all stacked neatly in the open. I was shocked to see how lackadaisical the guards were about showing us their area and letting me photograph it. The guards were obviously impressed with us. I doubt anyone had ever come to look at their area. I thought that this was a golden egg just waiting to be stolen. About a year after my tour ended, I read in an American newspaper article that munitions *were* being stolen from a storage area at BIAP. My suspicions were proven correct.

So, the BIAP areas that I toured showed me the following problems: first that derelict, empty buildings lay 300-1000 yards from Sather Air Base, with no fence nor wall between those open building and us. We did not know whether enemy personnel had access to these buildings to watch Sather Air Base or not. Second, BIAP itself was patrolled by a security company that had never been paid by the Iraqi government. Its security workers were nice guys who could never be able to stand up to a formidable opponent. Security checkpoints were essentially unguarded at night as most, if not all, the guards were asleep at their posts. Third, some workers at BIAP openly displayed support toward anti-government militias. How many of them would conspire to these militant fighters? Fourth, we came across storage buildings that were being watched and guarded by non-security company workers. Who were they and why were they so worried about these storage buildings? Fifth, there was a munitions area with live ammunition and new weapons which was only loosely guarded by four security workers. All of these problems deeply troubled me as I finished my tour of BIAP with my State Department friend. I had no way to effect changes in the security at BIAP, because it was under the control of the Iraqi Minister of Transportation. All of these issues came to mind as I thought of another serious problem brought to my attention from my predecessor.

During my changeover in late September 2006 my predecessor told me of worrisome issues being raised by our intelligence agency within the 447th AEG. Our intelligence collectors were actually members of an USAF Office of Special Investigation (OSI) flight within the 447th. Normally, the OSI investigates criminal actions of Air Force personnel within a USAF base. However, at Sather, they have another mission, which is to attempt to detect threats to our USAF installations. In Iraq, they mostly looked *outside* the organization toward illegal and dangerous activities that could possibly affect the 447th. The OSI was already generating numerous reports of the nefarious and illegal activity going on at BIAP. There were reports that planes were flying in weapons, money and anti-government people for the anti-government forces, mostly from Iran. My predecessor said that he had been getting reports for some time. I asked him who he had told about this bad news from BIAP. His answer was kind of ambiguous and I realized it would be up to me to sound the alarm regarding what was happening at BIAP.

My worries about the security situation in BIAP weren't over once I finished my alarming tour of the buildings there. About a week later I concluded my overall Sather Air Base inspection by visiting a structure that technically wasn't on the base – the BIAP Air Traffic Control Tower. This majestic structure rose 10 stories above the taxiways of BIAP and Sather Air Base. Again, it had been built to European standards and from a distance looked just like any modern building that you would see at any civilian airport in the U.S. or Europe.

The BIAP control tower was certainly vastly different than the short, squat and poorly constructed one that I was used to at Bagram Air Base in Afghanistan in 2002. So, I drove to the BIAP tower anticipating a top-notch structure with good security and facilities. I was, again, going to be vastly underwhelmed and shocked by every aspect of the control tower at BIAP.

Our little inspection group came to the tower in the morning. We were let into the parking lot via a two-man security gate for the tower and the Iraq equivalent of the FAA – a building next to the control tower. After going through the parking lot, we drove across the desert and were able to park right next to the ATC tower. This was a glaring vulnerability because an explosive laden truck could do the same thing and blow up the control tower merely by parking next to it, as was done at Khobar Towers, Saudi Arabia in 1996.

After driving right up to the tower we found that the only security measure for the entire structure was an old combination pad lock on the door. I asked who had the combination to this rickety, ancient door pad. As it turned out, everyone in the Iraqi FAA building had the combination – which meant scores of Iraqi workers, many without even the most rudimentary security background checks had the combination. There was no light or camera at the door pad. This was the lamest security I had ever seen at any military or civilian ATC tower anywhere, in the U.S. or abroad. As a pilot, I had often worked in military towers as the aircraft expert for our aircraft (called the Supervisor of Flying or SOF). I had worked in military towers in America, in Kuwait (as the only American in an all-Kuwaiti ATC crew), and finally in the "Wild West Show" that occurred at Bagram Air Base, Afghanistan. So, I was very familiar with the ATC procedures of a control tower.

After looking at the pitiful entry security for the BIAP tower, we entered the well-known security code into the creaky door lock. We were in. We walked up to the control tower elevator. The elevator looked harmless enough, until I tried to determine when this elevator had last been inspected for maintenance. There were no inspection stickers such as you see at elevators in America. I asked when someone, anyone, had inspected this elevator. Of course, the answer was that no one knew. We weren't going to ride that elevator anyway because I wanted to see what was on the rest of the floors of the control tower.

We started the slow walk up to each of the nine floors of the BIAP tower. What we found was derelict electrical equipment and vacant rooms on each floor. It was a repeat of the deserted buildings in BIAP - emptiness. Some windows had been left open on some floors and the pigeons had used the rooms for habitation, leaving years' worth of bird guano all over the place. We found no sign of people in the barren nine stories of the control tower; nor did we find any surveillance or security equipment on any of the unoccupied floors. This gave me great concern. Someone could enter the tower and set up an observation post on any of these floors without anyone on the top floor noticing it, because everyone took the elevator. Or they could set up a bomb site to destroy the entire structure! Eventually we arrived at the occupied last floor of the tower, the air traffic control station at the top. There finally, was the *only* security system for the entire structure, a small camera to look at us before we arrived at the busy end of this largely empty building.

We were viewed via a small video camera setup, buzzed in and arrived in the control tower. There were five Americans, all U.S. Air Force personnel, and about 15 civilian Iraqis in the tower. Four of the American controllers were intently facing toward the two runways at BIAP. They were standing next to the fifteen or so Iraqis doing the same thing. The fifth Air Force sergeant was the security monitor for the tower. He was the one who let us into the control cab of the tower.

I asked the Security Forces NCO about what he was looking at. He said the empty taxiways leading toward Sather Air Base. He was there to make sure no one launched a surprise attack against Sather from BIAP. I was happy he was there and that this was a security procedure that had been set up in the past. I then asked the Security Force NCO about the Iraqis in the tower. Who were the Iraqis? What were their names? Neither he nor anyone else in the tower could answer those questions. He said the Iraqis just showed up whenever they wanted, with no identification or a security check, and left at their leisure. This alarmed me in the extreme.

I asked several other questions which were answered with pitifully inadequate responses. How was the control tower powered? By a single generator and a bunch or power cables routed directly to the tower. Did the control tower have a backup? No. If there was a fire in the tower, how could the people get out if the elevator and stairwell were filled with smoke? No plan, no equipment. Did the tower have any backup radios? No. The more questions I asked, the more worried I got about how bad the situation was in the ATC tower. I won't even go into the problems with the air traffic flow into BIAP. Suffice to say that the helicopters and aircraft coming into BIAP had no plan for avoiding each other except via visual flight rules. Fine, except many flights, especially for the helicopters, were conducted at night under low light conditions where the pilots could not see each other! At night, many of the aircraft and helicopters, loaded with military passengers, flew with their lights turned off so as not to attract enemy gunfire from Baghdad. They would have great difficulty seeing each other, if at all.

Another issue came to light as we talked about how the BIAP tower worked. There was a tunnel that connected the terminal area to the tower. There were no security cameras in this tunnel, nor anything else to stop any one from moving from the terminal to the tower except the occasional locks, none of which were ever checked!

The ATC tower at BIAP, by itself, had major security problems. First, any IED-laden (improvised explosive device) vehicle could park right next to the building and destroy it. Second, the only security device covering the entry way to the tower was an ancient and flimsy combination lock whose code was known by every Iraqi who worked in the tower, rendering it useless. There were no cameras or lights by the entry doors. Third, the first nine floors of the tower were fallow and empty. The floors were never patrolled or checked for weapons or bombs. Fourth, we did not know who the Iraqis working in the tower really were and there was no security screening to get into the control cab at the top floor. Fifth, all the Americans in the tower were focused on looking *outside*. Either toward the runways for aircraft / helicopters or the taxiways for foreign intruders. No one was concerned with the security of the tower cab, especially toward the five, ten or fifteen Iraqis who might pose a weapons or bombs threat. Sixth, there was a tunnel from the terminal that led directly to the tower into which guns, money and possible terrorists were flying in daily according to my OSI team and for which there was absolutely no security.

Frankly, I left the tower *shaken* by the serious security and air traffic control issues. BIAP was the premier civilian airport for the country. Sather Air Base was the second busiest military airfield in Iraq. Yet the security measures for the control tower were worse than Joe's airport in Podunk, USA. I couldn't make changes to this situation unilaterally because the Iraqis controlled BIAP! Baghdad International Airport was a civilian Iraqi airport and the workers in the tower were employees of the Iraqi government. I would have to move slyly, diplomatically and quickly to correct the security and air traffic control problems at BIAP.

I would also have to be secretive about making changes to the security problems in the BIAP control tower. If the anti-government forces discovered even *one* of the security problems at BIAP they could cause huge damage and gain an enormous amount of publicity for just a small amount of risk. For instance, they could sneak a team of terrorists into the tower and kidnap our Air Force personnel while holding the tower as hostage! Since we had no tower backup, both BIAP and Sather would be closed to flights. The level of negative media attention would be enormous for such a dramatic event. The same effect would happen if they just blew up the tower. My view, through my Vietnam War prism, was that the enemy would jump at the chance to get such a publicity bonanza!

My real question was, given the operational and propaganda risk, why we continued for three and a half years with this incredibly flimsy security setup and the dangerous air traffic flow into BIAP? Upon arriving back at my office, I began to write down all of the problems at BIAP and the control tower on my white board. Some issues had to be dealt with immediately and some would take more time to fix. I was genuinely afraid of the lack of security in BIAP and the tower.

Immediately, I had the Security Forces squadron push their patrols right up to the borderline with BIAP. We could not assume that the British security company would provide us with any degree of protection if there was an enemy intrusion. Whereas the first problem required a show of force, the second one required us to be much more cunning. This was the issue of the Iraqi personnel working in the ATC tower. Who were they and how good were they? Our people had no idea on the first question and their air traffic control skills were fair to very poor. My big concern was that the bad guys could sneak a few terrorists with weapons in with a daily work crew and then there would be hell to pay.

My initial solution was to insert an armed USAF person into our work crew in the ATC tower. While everyone else was looking outside the tower at aircraft or the taxiways, this person would only be concerned with what was going on *inside* the tower. They would watch the Iraqis, looking for anything suspicious. This armed person would also keep a secret log of who was working in tower for the Iraqis. We instituted a nametag system in the tower for the Iraqis, mainly so we knew what names to put into our stealthy logbook. This security person in the tower would ensure every person in the tower wore a nametag during their work shift. Finally, we built a notebook just for the Iraqis with their photographs in it. We asked the Iraqis to fill out details about themselves, such as their age, address, marital status, children and the like. Interestingly, the Iraqis were very enthusiastic about this notebook and the nametag system. I realized, that up to this point, no one had shown even the least bit of interest in them, not even to learn their names.

However, when it came to filling the position for the security guard for the tower, I got surprising pushback from the Security Forces squadron. Although not staffed for this position, I wanted the security monitor in the tower to come from their squadron. They were security trained and this task was right up their alley. However, the commander of the squadron said that he didn't have *anyone* of his 100+ personnel to spare. I quickly surmised that the commander did not think that this monitor job was important or that the situation in the tower was as dire as I believed it to be. This was very disappointing, but I felt this to be an urgent requirement and needed it to happen right away with enthusiastic people performing the role who both understood its importance and were properly trained and equipped. So, I requested the other squadrons to ask for volunteers to man this position. I got plenty of keen volunteers, gathered them all together and I personally briefed them on the seriousness of the tower situation. I wanted to make sure that the workers there were passionate and eager for this secret duty.

My pep talk worked and these volunteers were pumped up. Within a day or two of my visit to the tower, the new system was instituted and they began keeping the secret log of Iraqi workers, the security monitoring, the daily nametag drill and finally the Iraqi name book. The daytime security volunteers did all of the jobs I just outlined. The night tower security guard had a different job. Since the Iraqi tower controllers only worked during the daytime (BIAP was only opened during the hours of daylight) I had a completely different task for the night guards. They were to patrol the nine derelict and empty stories of the tower and look for any subtle changes, such as the storage of weapons or explosives anywhere in the tower. Again, we were doing this activity without the knowledge of the Iraqi FAA, since this was an Iraqi building.

Perhaps these guards and this secret activity may seem paranoid now, but we were at the height of the anti-American and anti-government activity in Baghdad in 2006. At the time, I had no idea what the state of the security was at BIAP or in the tower. I did not know which workers might be supporters of the militant forces, as evidenced by the presence of the JAM stickers on the lockers, or how far they might go to attack Sather AB or the tower. We found out that information only by a cunning plan which I will discuss later in this chapter.

While we dealt with the most dangerous elements of BIAP security problems within the first day or two after learning of them, we could now start to build a long-term plan for making Sather AB safer. We began to look at the overall level of security at Sather AB in relation to rocket attacks, which we were now getting a couple times a week or a surprise terrorist attack from BIAP. The rocket attacks were a fairly consistent factor, although they were landing all over the base, albeit most of which was empty. My concern with the rocket attacks was what would happen if one exploded in the tent city or if there was a concentrated attack with a salvo of rockets. During one of my visits to Balad AB, which was the biggest Air Force base in Iraq, I saw such a concentrated attack of six mortar rounds against the base. Of course, there the C-RAM (Counter Rocket, Artillery, Mortar) worked and the 20 mm Gatling gun system, with its 6,000 rounds per minute of fire, shot down at least one of the mortar shells in the group!

I had to expect the worst from the rocket attacks and hope for the best. The first issue with the rocket attacks dealt with the training of all the people of Sather. As I said before, all of the Air Force people at Sather came from over 60 bases throughout the world. I asked the people that I addressed in the "Right Start" introductory briefings what their level of training was. The level of experience and training varied wildly. Based on the feedback that I received, my estimation was that 20% of the personnel had very poor or no training at all. We needed to get everyone, including the Army, British and civilians up to the same level of training and focus.

The first piece of training that I wanted everyone in the base to receive was combat first aid. In the USAF, first aid is called "Self-Aid and Buddy Care (SABC)". We quickly instituted classes taught by the best teachers on Sather AB – the doctors from our base hospital. These doctors were mostly surgeons, so I greatly appreciated that they kept their briefings on a layman level. Given the cases they'd had to treat, the doctors understood better than most, the seriousness of the rocket threat to Sather and they made great instructors for our people.

The interesting thing about combat first aid was that since "9/11" (Sept 11, 2001) there had been a revolution in treatment of battle wounds. The combat tourniquet was now the primary technique used for *any* serious bleeding injury – either self-applied or done by a buddy. Other new tools included a compression bandage called the "Israeli Bandage" and a powder used for really extensive wounds called "Quick Clot". These three items were just a part of a USAF-wide distribution of Self-Aid and Buddy Care (SABC) kits worn by all Airmen called the "IFAK" – Individual First Aid Kit. The advanced technology, combined with the new level of combat first-aid knowledge among the American military were some of the key reasons that so many of our wounded were saved compared to previous wars.

I was a huge believer in the proper use of the IFAK because it might be the only way to save a life. As I told everyone at Sather, "Imagine that you are walking in an isolated part of the base, with a friend, when a mortar hits near you both. Your friend is now bleeding to death – do you have the knowledge to save his/her life?" I wanted everyone at Sather to have this level of combat first aid training and I did my best to ensure that they got it.

SABC classes became mandatory for all the Air Force personnel at Sather. Prime consideration was given to real hands-on practice with all the major parts of the IFAK pouch. We practiced these both during the day and, especially, during the night hours, which I considered to be the prime time for such attacks. Eventually, I was able to convince the civilian contractors to take this first aid training, since they were part of our world at Sather. Most of the contractors were women who worked at the local Base Exchange (BX), a small, trailer-sized operation on the base. The workers became more motivated to take this IFAK training after a rocket hit an Army ammunition depot about six miles from Sather in early October. Massive explosions from the depot went off throughout the night and created a sense of urgency, which facilitated my goals of getting as many people as possible to take this critical training.

The next new security technology for all personnel at Sather AB was body armor. Since medieval times there has always been the hope that armor would stop the main infantry weapon of the day, be it arrows or bullets. In fact, gunpowder and bullets largely ended the wearing of armor suits in Europe over 500 years ago. In modern times the best protection a soldier could get was what was called a "flak jacket", which was intended to protect the wearer from pieces of shrapnel from an exploding shell. Shrapnel is the term used for the jagged pieces of the metal thrown off from the casings of rocket, artillery or mortar shells as they explode. Shrapnel is very dangerous because the explosive charge propels these metal fragments at great speed from the explosion. For instance, a single enemy 107mm rocket that hit 30 yards from a C-5 aircraft in December, 2006 at Sather AB put over 30 shrapnel holes in the aircraft. Some of them penetrated the aluminum skin of the aircraft. One fragment went through both sides of aircraft.

By the time of our tour in Iraq, there had been tremendous improvements in the quality and capabilities of the latest body armor – it could now stop multiple enemy AK-47 bullets and it was also effective against shrapnel. This bullet-proof body armor protected the entire upper torso of the wearer. The downside of this tremendous military capability was that the complete set of body armor weighed about 65 pounds (29.5 kilos). Since the people serving at Sather AB were of both sexes, different sizes and varying degrees of physical conditioning I felt everyone needed to understand the challenge of wearing body armor.

As in the case of the IFAK first aid kit, it was necessary to get used to wearing the heavy body armor. I had gone through much the same challenge at Bagram AB, Afghanistan in 2002-3. There we also experienced rocket attacks and I needed to adapt to that threat. At Sather AB I knew what to expect and could *anticipate* events rather than waiting for them to occur. I realized that all the Sather personnel were going to have to wear body armor and that the vast majority (unlike the Army or Marines) had not worn it before. So, I organized an event to drive home the difficulties of this amazing but cumbersome body armor.

I had everyone in the 447th AEG run or walk 1.5 miles on the little track in our tent city, while wearing a full set of body armor and a Kevlar helmet. Now for the Marine and Army readers, this event may seem rather lame. But if we're going to make warriors out of airmen, you have to move forward with small steps at first. I foresaw that there would be a lot of complaining about this event since it was certainly a first for the USAF. The griping was substantial but I didn't care. Instead of just talking about the warrior ethos we were going to live it. After the combat first aid training, the body armor run/walk was our second step towards a base prepared for combat.

I scheduled the run/walk on October 1st, which just happened to be my 50th birthday. What a way to celebrate it! We had many hundreds of Air Force personnel attending the event, as planned. I gave a pep-talk speech before the event and said that everyone had to finish, because we all had to get used to wearing the body armor. I said that I would be setting the 'slow run pace' and that people could go faster or slower as long as they completed the, admittedly, meager distance. I also stated that someday they could brag about how they were the only ones in the Air Force to have finished such an event.

Since there were various whiney complaints that "we could die" during this event, I had our enthusiastic medical personnel from the hospital lining the track to make sure that there were no problems from their end. We started the race and the personnel in the best physical condition raced ahead, some even burdened down with their rifles. I definitely set the slow running pace but was able to at least finish without walking. After doing so, I was able to congratulate many of the slower runners or walkers. This was about getting comfortable with the heavy body armor and finding if one needed to get in better shape to carry it. That's what happened – I and many others realized that we needed to hit the gym to be ready for when we might need to wear the body armor for real. When we actually had to wear the body armor over six separate time throughout our tour, there were no complaints because folks were ready for it via this run/walk event.

The third piece of training to be ready for the "Eye of the Hurricane", i.e., rocket attacks from Baghdad, was to practice a base-wide rocket attack scenario. In the Air Force, these drills are called Operational Readiness Exercises (ORE's) to get ready for the dreaded Operational Readiness Inspection (ORI). These both are practiced on a regular basis by all Air Force, Reserve and Air National Guard (ANG) units. In fact, the ORE and ORI are one of the reasons that Air Guard and Reserve units can deploy overseas almost as quickly as active duty units. My own Air Guard A-10 unit deployed to Iraq in 2003 with only one week's notice.

Interestingly, the Operational Readiness Exercises of combat units *in the United States* assumes that the enemy attack would use chemical weapons, even though they have not been used against American troops since 1918 (in France during World War I). So much time in these OREs and ORIs was spent in hot, anti-chemical suits and masks. We were not going to assume chemical weapons at Sather, but the much more likely scenario of a concentrated rocket attack. Fortunately, the enemy would occasionally send us a *real* rocket explosion, which greatly motivated our Airmen to training toward that threat. Also, every night there was a great deal of gunfire from one of the nearby Iraqi Special Forces Camps, again providing the backdrop for training for a real attack on Sather Air Base.

We organized the first readiness exercise in early October. I knew that it would not go well, since some of the Airmen had never been in an ORE before. I followed much the same plan that I had used at Bagram AB in Afghanistan when we came under rocket attacks there. I would place fake "casualties" all over the base to simulate rocket shrapnel injuries. These casualties would be made up in fake combat injuries, called moulage. Most would look and show blood injuries just like the real thing. Many of the actual moulage casualty players would be the doctors and nurses who would grade the combat first aid as performed by the responders.

As the exercise date approached we began to look at aspects of the tent city and work areas. There were no bomb shelters anywhere on the base. We had no litters (portable body carriers) anywhere to help move casualties. We had no portable first aid kits to go with the litters. I immediately began to order these items from the USAF procurement system.

Everything in this first readiness exercise was scripted. The time and date of it was announced in advance. It was in the daytime. People had access to their IFAK. The only thing we couldn't simulate was explosions but for that we used smoke grenades to get people fired up. From the beginning the first exercise was largely a mess. People didn't know where to go, we didn't have enough bomb shelters, since we started with none, and, worst of all, we didn't have a good plan for searching for casualties. If this had been a real attack, many of our casualties would have died before they were found and attended to. At Bagram AB, Afghanistan our Air Force camp was small enough to search for casualties on foot, but here we needed to use small vehicles called "gators", four wheel all-terrain vehicles. I was not disappointed with the results for this first exercise, since we were trying to put so many pieces together for the first time. But I wanted the next exercise to be much smoother and more successful.

I got a great deal of help from the doctors and nurses from our base hospital. Not only had they taught the initial combat first aid classes, but they also acted as the fake casualties, spread all over the base, with different moulage patterns, simulating different wounds. As our Air Force personnel dealt with the first aid situation the real doctors and nurses could critique them on their techniques. Another area in which the doctors took charge was the placement of the litters and first aid kits throughout the base. I was very impressed with the energy that they applied to these security tasks. In general, the base population worked hard to get better at the readiness exercises, especially since we made them more difficult as time went on.

The second readiness exercise was vastly more successful than the first, although we again held it during the day, with plenty of notice. Because of the doctor's efforts, we now had base-wide litter and first aid stations. This was due to the energetic leadership of Colonel William Dodson, who led the medical unit. He and his doctors were real superstars in preparing Sather for a disaster. Civil Engineering had also worked diligently to place the newly arrived concrete bomb shelters that we bought throughout the base. Everyone had a set shelter, where roll call was to be taken, so that we could keep track of all of our personnel. It was really gratifying to see it all come together, especially since the first exercise had not gone very well.

We didn't rest on our laurels after the second readiness exercise. I anticipated that a planned, enemy rocket attack would happen at night, since less of our Baghdad security forces would be there to react to its launch. Also, even with NVGs, it is harder to operate at night. So, we needed to have an exercise at night to make sure that we were ready for that possible event.

Sather Air Base had its third readiness exercise at night in late October, 2006. Just to put this into perspective, *no other Air Base in Iraq* conducted even *one* full-length ORE during our tour. Balad tried to have one and it lasted about 10 minutes. Each time we did these exercises, we improved on previous results. Our casualties were found quicker and taken care of with combat first aid efficiently. By the third exercise we had completed the procurement and placement of over 100 brand new bomb shelters throughout the base. By our third exercise everyone knew where to go and we had accountability once people had filled up each bomb shelter.

The final test for our readiness exercises was to be an *unannounced* one; no forewarning and at night with no radio communication in the darkness of the desert. This exercise would be as realistic possible in simulating an actual night time attack from positions in BIAP or a rocket attack from Baghdad. This trial would be in early November and was to be the real test of our readiness in case of an actual attack.

By now, I had convinced both the Army, British and civilian contractors on Sather to take our "Right Start" USAF training, including my commanders brief. My argument for this training was simple – we were all in it together at Sather AB and we must depend on each other for combat first aid and threat response. I also threw in incentives, such as the Army being able to use our vehicle maintenance building, in order to sweeten the pot for this training. So, for the first time the entire base population would participate in this readiness exercise. Again, we were the only base in Iraq to hold readiness exercises during our tour and certainly the only one to include other services in our practice.

At exactly 2100 (9:00 pm) on an early November night, I launched our last readiness exercise. I said we were under attack and for the base to quickly and quietly proceed to their bomb shelters in body armor and helmets. Even with the other services being involved for the first time, this practice base attack was the smoothest yet. At exactly 9:42 pm, I had the "all accounted for" messages from all the bomb shelters throughout Sather. To be sure that everyone was actually doing what was expected, I visited random bomb shelters throughout the base and took pictures there. I was incredibly proud of all the personnel at Sather because they had taken this training seriously. They had taken the warrior ethos to heart.

Early in November I was visited by the Deputy Commander of CENTAF (Central Command – Air Force), MG Holland. During the visit, I gave him my evolving briefing on the security issues at BIAP. Part of the briefing concerned the separate living quarters for the EOD and Fire Department, where they had been for 3 and 1/2 years. I was unhappy since their combined building was only 300 yards from the derelict buildings on BIAP. There was no protection in the EOD/Fire building from a surprise attack from BIAP. I was concerned about this and said so in the briefing. Holland then said to me and my staff, "Take care of this [security] situation". After he left, I met with the Commander of Civil Engineering (CE) on the relocation of the Fire Company and the Explosive Ordnance Disposal (EOD) squadron. The commander had attended this meeting with MG Holland and listened as I was told to deal with the security problem there. I was shocked when the commander said to me, "Can we just ignore that order from the general?". Wow! I was shocked that a USAF Major would say something like that in front of his CE staff. Not only did he want me to disobey a general, who gave me a lawful order, but one that concerned a problem/solution that I had identified!

I answered Robert hotly, "Robert (not his real name), can you make the call to the families if someone is killed because of this security issue?" The CE commander was more concerned about EOD and the Fire units losing their little "club house" away from the main camp, over the threat of a surprise attack from BIAP. Little did I realize that this short encounter would affect my career. In this case, I wasn't going to waste my time trying to convince anyone of my wishes, I simply ordered them to do it and let them handle the details. I gave CE two days to move the Fire Department to the main part of Sather and two weeks to relocate the EOD squadron to a remote part of Sather in a new area. Fortunately, the CE Commander met both of the time restrictions for the relocation and I sent an email with attached pictures to MG Holland saying that his security wishes had been fulfilled.

Over my tour, we made Sather AB into a veritable fortress. Besides the combat first aid training and four readiness exercises that was accomplished with all the Air Force, Army, British and civilian workers we bought concrete structures to build up the physical infrastructure of the base. The centerpiece of this fortification of Sather was adding over 1500 wall pieces called "Alaskan barriers". An Alaskan barrier is a physical self-supporting wall of over twelve feet of concrete and steel. It is capable of stopping shrapnel, bullets or rockets - which was its purpose. The Civil Engineers did a great job over the course of our tour of building walls to place real barriers between us, BIAP and Baghdad rocket attacks. The Alaskan barriers added to the security of Sather and limited any potential harm from rocket attacks in the future.

Another step toward increasing the defenses at Sather was the adding of over 100 concrete and steel bunkers throughout the base. Each bunker could hold 20-30 persons wearing full body armor. The bunkers could survive a direct hit from a rocket and were placed in areas where people worked, relaxed and slept. Finally, at different strategic locations, that were determined by the hard-working doctors of our base hospital, we placed litters and extra first aid kits. The additions of the 1500 Alaskan barriers, the 100 above-ground bomb shelters and the first aid and litter stations truly made Sather into a far more hardened base than what we had inherited when we arrived.

Except for the rocket that hit next to a C-5 and another that hit the base of a building in New Al Muthana, the Iraqi base right next to Sather AB – 800 yards away, and several rockets that scored direct hits on a BIAP passenger terminal, we had few serious *exploding* rockets attacks near anything important at Sather AB during our tour. By the way, none of these aforementioned rockets set off the C-RAM system. We also experienced quite a few enemy dud rockets, as evidenced by large dust clouds, but no explosions.

During our AEF tour, the BX parking lot at one of the nearby Army bases was struck by two large rocket explosions. After these strikes, there were people running, taking pictures, laughing, crying, etc., but no one responded quickly to several actual American casualties. Who organized the scene and performed combat first aid before the ambulance arrived? That's right, a couple USAF personnel from Sather AB, who used the training that we had given them. Which was the point – USAF Self Aid and Buddy Care or combat first aid can be used in real life once your tour is over and you return to the civilian world. So, although not specifically needed at Sather AB, I'm still glad we insisted on conducting all of the training for combat first-aid and our four readiness exercises. I would happily be accused of over-training, rather than face the opposite, which was the case before or after our tour.

Another interesting security tale happened on one of the several visits by U.S. Secretary of State, Condoleezza Rice, to Iraq in the fall of 2006. Only two persons at Sather AB knew of the Secretary's visit that day. I and my protocol officer were the only ones who knew she was coming because this was a very closely guarded secret. About an hour before her arrival, I began to get several disturbing reports from different locations. First, was the discovery of a possible unexploded IED on BIAP. Then, there was the explosion of a rocket in an empty area of Sather AB. The third was the discovery of a group of large propane tanks bundled together next to the high security wall and road directly outside Sather AB. I received these calls within 15 minutes of each other and thirty minutes before her arrival. Were all they related? Could this be the start of a coordinated attack centered on her landing at Sather AB? I didn't know, but we needed time to sort out these individual security threats immediately. I quickly called the tower and told them *not* allow her aircraft to land. As of now, she was on a temporary hold from landing. Her aircraft had plenty of fuel to hold above Baghdad, so that was not an issue.

Almost immediately, I started to receive calls on my classified telephone line from worried State Department officials. Cryptically they asked me if I knew who was on the aircraft that I was holding up from landing. I said that I knew who was onboard, but that we had security problems at Sather AB / BIAP and that until it was resolved, I wasn't going to allow her to land. What I didn't say was that while I was talking to them I couldn't get to the bottom of these related or unrelated security problems. We looked at each of these problems intently. The most worrisome was the group of large propane tanks latched together outside our Sather walls. This could have been a way to blow a huge hole in our fortification. But there was no detonator or trigger devise on the tanks and they were found to be left there by a truck that had broken down. They were guarded and eventually removed. The supposed IED in BIAP was found to be a fake by our EOD Airmen and the rocket explosion was just one of those that hit us every couple of days. After being held from landing for 30 minutes, I gave permission for her military plane to land at Sather AB. Except for the frantic calls from the State Department minions who think that landing in Baghdad during the height of a real war is the same as arriving at Andrews Air Force base outside Washington, DC, this was how the system is supposed to work. The delayed landing made the newspapers of the day but that was the end of it.

As far as the other crises of our time, the handling of the Iraqi workers in the BIAP tower, ended up being a brilliant overall success. Here's how it happened: we kept up the daily nametag drill, which the Iraqis liked. Eventually, we determined that the reason that so many of the Iraqis were coming up to the tower was because they wanted to get paid. We sent some of the most poorly-trained Iraqi controllers back to school for much needed refresher ATC training. We then began issuing *our own* security ID cards, which the controllers needed to get into *their tower*. The Iraqis liked this because they wanted to be safe also. We had each Iraqi controller fill out extensive security paperwork, which we vetted through the Central Intelligence Agency (CIA) – with whom we maintained close ties with during my tour. By the end of the tour all the Iraqis had been vetted by us. Although we found some anti-government sympathizers among the controllers, we did not think any rose to the level of committing malicious acts.

Our nightly patrols of the tower confirmed to me that no one was using the tower to store weapons or explosives. But no one knew that we were doing the patrols except us, so "better safe than sorry". That was the motto for all the security measures that we handled at Sather AB during our tour.

We investigated the underground tunnel going between the terminal and the ATC tower. It was filled with old, nasty water and was NOT a travel conduit used by anyone. Not only did we change the locks for the entrances for the tunnel (to which only we had the keys) but I also had our Civil Engineering people *weld* the gates of the tunnel shut. So that secret avenue to the tower was closed.

We added monitoring cameras to the outside entry doors of the control tower. We ordered an updated door lock system and an emergency fire escape system for the ATC tower. It eventually arrived after my departure, as I later saw a picture of a man using the system to drop 10 stories from the control tower to the ground in an USAF publication in the summer of 2007. That's how long it took to fix some of the bigger problems at Sather. It was simply "adding another brick to the house".

The strategic security problems at BIAP prompted me to develop a powerful briefing on the subject in October, 2006. That briefing and its' ultimate ramifications will be covered in Chapter 8.

In summary, I tried to anticipate all the security issues that could possibly happen at Sather AB, based on the information that I had. Then we designed and implemented countermeasures to cope with these threats. I did not care whether the countermeasures had ever been done there before. My job was to try to bring everyone home safely *during my tour*, regardless of how much training we had to do to counterbalance the threat. Our Sather AB personnel could be proud that they were the first ones to achieve that level of training in Iraq for facing the real-world threats that we encountered. We were the first ones to receive combat first aid in theater, taught by doctors. This training later saved lives on a nearby Army base. We were the only base to accomplish even one Operational Readiness Exercise, much less *four* full-length ones, including two at night with one being without any notice.

In the end, it wasn't just the lives that we saved by doing this security training and taking the many steps that we took, it was about the lives that we *would have saved* by our attention to the threats during our tour. I made a promise to my people that I would get them through the tour, if they followed my lead. I looked at every security problem from the worst-case scenario. Then, we trained to negate those threats.

CHAPTER SEVEN
DRAINING THE USAF DUMPING GROUND
– PERSONNEL ISSUES

During my tour at the 447th AEG, some substantial issues made themselves evident immediately, while others took time to surface. I had missed the opportunity to brief all of the 447th personnel at my initial "Right Start" briefing. For the people that I did brief, I made it crystal clear that General Order 1A violations would be handled in theater (i.e., at Sather Air Base) and that *all infringements* would be prosecuted immediately and with full punishment. I hoped that my predecessor had said the same thing because I felt that was the best way to handle these types of issues.

To escape the many morale and discipline issues of the Vietnam War, it was my firm belief, and those of the other commanders in Iraq and Afghanistan, that we needed to run a tight ship. Not Draconian, but strict, as far as GO1A violations went. It wasn't as if the deployed USAF personnel had to give up beer for a whole year, for this was only a 4-6 month AEF tour. So, everyone had been warned, on multiple occasions, to steer clear of the GO1A issues. Yet, they occurred anyway. I had few discipline problems at Bagram AB, Afghanistan, a much tougher duty station and for a longer period. However, at Sather, they began popping up as soon as I assumed command.

My first discipline problem came from an unexpected person – a high-ranking officer who was also a unit commander. When I first arrived to Sather my predecessor briefed me that the Security Forces (SF) Squadron Commander had given him a number of problems – almost enough to warrant sending him home. Since this SF officer had only been at Sather for two weeks and also because my predecessor was a pretty laid back dude, I wondered what possibly could have happened to arrive at this drastic conclusion. Evidently, the SF commander wouldn't follow the camp rules, was generally a poor example for his Airmen and had a big mouth. Great. I was already beginning to get an inkling of enormous security issues at Sather AB / BIAP and all I needed was to have a disgruntled commander in charge of my security forces.

After my very first staff meeting, I sat down with the SF Squadron Commander in my office. I told him that perhaps he had gotten off on the wrong foot with the former commander, but that I intended to give him a fresh start. In the modern terminology, this was a "reset" meeting. I said we were both graduates of the U.S. Air Force Academy, and that I needed him to be part of the team that provided solutions at Sather AB. He seemed to agree and I hoped that I had resolved this problem quickly and quietly. I was wrong and his poor performance would metasticize itself into his unit and its people.

Despite our meeting, this officer continued to ooze discontent and pushback. At every staff meeting, he was the biggest and loudest naysayer as we struggled to fix the many dangerous problems at Sather. He often disagreed with potential solutions to critical security issues, yet offered no solutions of his own to address problems that had been identified and agreed upon by all the other units. During these meetings, he had an irritating ability to take discussions on a tangential path instead of addressing the core threat or any solutions. I quickly began to understand my predecessor's complaints about him. But the biggest problem was with the overall performance of the security forces personnel. They looked bad and were the worst performers in the 447th. Their problems as a unit resulted from his overall bad attitude and his failure to set a good example. I began pondering over what to do about him.

When I flew to Balad AB, in early October, for my second meeting with BG Rand and his staff, I told him that I was having issues with this particular SF commander. At this conference, I was struck by difference between the Security Forces personnel at Balad – looking and sounding sharp, motivated and gung ho, versus the lackadaisical and slack personnel at Sather. During this visit, all of the base commanders gave briefings on their facility and Groups to the USAF leadership in Iraq. We were already at a very fast pace at Sather, so my briefing covered what we had been doing and was well-received. Rand gave a briefing of his own and then said something important, "If you have problem personnel, just send them home". That statement lit a small fire in my belly regarding my SF commander.

I returned from Balad with a specific task in mind for our Sather SF personnel, one that would allow me to compare their performance with what I had observed at Balad. I wanted my SF personnel to be able to give a report at his/her post, upon being questioned, that would include the condition of the post and the threats to which it was exposed. I had seen SF personnel at Balad give this report to their commanders with pride and efficiency. Could we do the same thing at Sather? I tasked the SF commander with making this happen for his people. Then I waited to see what would occur.

In fact, nothing happened. The SF commander did not think the report issue was useful or that it would build pride in their mission, and, thus, did not require his people to do it. I was very disappointed that this task wasn't fulfilled but not surprised when it didn't happen. The commander had a negative attitude, which reflected in his people and the unit's performance. With the huge security issues at Sather AB and BIAP, I didn't have any confidence in him to lead our base security forces if a real attack or crisis occurred.

Throughout late September / early October I continued to examine my options for dealing with this commander's continued marginal performance. I met with him privately several times, trying to determine what his issues were and to get him on board and his unit back on track. It turned out that he was upset because he had been passed over twice for promotion at his home unit. I couldn't get him to set his disappointment over not being promoted aside and focus on operations here Iraq. Instead, he allowed his resentment at being passed over and then sent to Iraq to fester. He adopted an obstructionist attitude in all our staff meetings. Whenever a security issue came up his position was to "argue, pontificate and do nothing". I continually encourage discussion and a lively exchange of ideas. But with lives at stake, I couldn't allow an endless debating society. We needed solutions and successes. What was required was a bold leader to help me sort out and eliminate the security problems at Sather, not ignore them.

This man's attitude was a recipe for disaster. He continually made excuses and never offered any solutions for improving either his people's or his unit's substandard performance. This SF unit compared very unfavorably with what I had seen at Balad and also at Bagram. I worried that if his unit was this bad now, what would it be like after another five months of his disheartened leadership?

Removing a Lt Colonel and a unit commander from a combat base would be a very big deal because of his rank, experience and position. We were also taking this drastic action based on less than three weeks of observation under my leadership. In addition, he need to be rapidly replaced from a stateside USAF SF unit, outside the normal AEF rotation system meaning his replacement would be someone who hadn't planned on being deployed. In addition to that, I was also concerned about the underlying tension between the ANG and the active duty USAF.

Ever since Operation DESERT STORM (1990-91), the USAF has frequently used the Air Reserve Component (ARC), the term used to refer to the combination of the ANG and AFR unit in combat. Unlike the Army, where Reserve or Guard units must spend 5-6 months or more to spin up for their deployments, the ANG and AFR units can deploy without additional training. My own A-10 ANG unit had been deployed *seven times* to Southwest Asia between 1995 and 2008. Most of the pilots from our unit had previously served in the active duty USAF or other services. There was a qualitative difference between active duty and ARC units. For any given career field or occupational specialty, across the board, ARC member had roughly three times the experience compared to their younger, generally less experienced active duty counterparts. In the A-10 community our ANG aircraft were in far better mechanical shape than those of the active duty. This was because an ANG mechanic may have worked on the same aircraft for 15-25 years. Yet, there was a real tendency in combat locations for the active duty personnel to *initially* look down on the older, but more experienced ANG personnel. They always assume that our Guard people only trained for their flying missions just one weekend a month! It's the old 'National Guard' or citizen-soldier stigma.

In 2002, I once had a commanding general, whom I greatly admired, ask me before I went to Bagram AB, Afghanistan, how we Guardsmen stayed proficient in the A-10 fighter aircraft? The real question he was asking was how did we stay current and well-trained in a front-line aircraft on just two days a month worth of training? But that's the *Army* National Guard way. In the *Air* National Guard, the pilots average 6-10 days a month training and flying. That, combined with the high level of experience of our people, made for flying units equal or greater in capability to their younger and leaner active duty ones.

So, there is a bias against members of the Air National Guard and Air Force Reserve in the active duty USAF. Sort of a "second-class citizen" mentality, always seemingly present below the surface. The truth is that members of the Air Guard, like myself, understood the active duty and ANG because we've served in both. But the active duty definitely does NOT understand the Air Guard. My goal at both Bagram and Sather was to perform at a level as equal to or better than my active duty equivalent. So, when it came to the decision to remove an active duty Lt Colonel from his command at Sather AB by an Air National Guard Colonel I couldn't be sure how it would be received.

I assumed that my decision to remove this Lt Colonel would instigate a visit from CENTAF that would cause *either* the Security Forces commander to be taken away from Iraq *or myself*. When I received an unrelated call from BG Rand in mid-October, this problem had reached the crisis point. Either I lived with all the negative aspects of this lousy commander for the next five months or I did something about it. It was him or me.

So, I reluctantly pulled that proverbial trigger. I told General Rand that I wanted the SF commander to be removed from his position. I knew that this would be a 'battle to the death' with only one of us surviving. However, I had reached the end of my rope with this commander, I had serious security concerns at Sather and I could not afford an SF commander who would not address those concerns. General Rand said that he would have to call Lt General North (CENTAF Commander) that day about this request to remove this senior active duty officer from command. This was a serious charge and would be dealt with immediately.

The next day, I was told to expect a visit from the commander of the CENTAF Security Forces. As soon as this serious and upright Colonel arrived, I sat down with him and discussed the numerous substantive issues that I had with this officer. I briefed him on the many security issues of Sather and BIAP, including our occasional rocket attacks. I asked him to contact my predecessor and get his concerns regarding the commander. I also asked that he visit the SF squadron and talk to them there. I then awaited the verdict. After two days, the colonel from CENTAF agreed with me. He had observed numerous personnel issues and agreed that the SF squadron was being poorly led.

The next day we put a plan into action. Although I regretted that I couldn't influence this particular commander to focus on Iraq, he couldn't overcome his bitterness over his own floundering career. But I had no other option under the circumstances than to relieve him of command. I had the CENTAF Colonel and a SF senior NCO sit outside my office. I called the SF commander to my office and in a closed-door session, told him that he was being relieved, effective immediately. I also explained my reasons for relieving him, which should have been no surprise to him. He was shocked and angry and I was a little nervous because he was wearing his sidearm. Our terse but respectful conversation lasted about five to ten minutes. There was no profanity or acrimony. When we finished, he stood up but did not salute me, as was the standard courtesy for any meeting with the commander. Then he was relieved of his firearm and escorted to his quarters to pack his personal effects and was flown out the same day.

I visited the SF unit immediately after he had left and addressed the entire squadron. I stated that their commander's removal was not their fault and did not reflect negatively on them. I told them how critical they were to the mission of Sather AB – particularly in light of the problems we were seeing at BIAP. I said that they were to follow the leadership of the deputy until a new commander arrived at Sather.

Less than a month later, the new SF replacement commander arrived. He had volunteered with zero-notice to come to Sather to fill this post. His name was LtCol Stephen Mezhir and he was a fantastic addition to our team. He was everything the previous commander had not been – positive, energetic and a real role model for his people. He was a definite contributor to the security issues of Sather and a fun guy to have around. I had him brief BG Rand the next time he was at Sather and discovered that they already knew each other from a previous assignment. Most of all, LtCol Mezhir helped get the SF squadron prepared for the threats at Sather and began to deal with a number of personnel issues. In the end, it was worth all the pain, angst and anxiety of relieving the previous commander to bring a true leader and role model, like Mezhir, to the field.

The extensive drama of removing the SF Squadron commander, was just the start of a resolving the discipline problems in the 447th. Unfortunately, many of these personnel issues occurred in the SF squadron. It's easy to understand how the deleterious attitude of a disgruntled commander could spread like a cancer to his subordinates over the course of an AEF tour. Unfortunately, that's exactly what happened.

The Achilles Heel of the USAF AEF concept was the mixture of personnel from 60 bases across the globe. Often units would deploy together, but for many positions no one had ever trained or worked together. Most units, assigned with providing AEF members, did the right thing but a few took advantage of the AEF system. Some sent their best people, some sent volunteers and some used the AEF system as a garbage disposal.

A very few USAF units abused the AEF system by sending us their "problem children", people with prior serious discipline issues or who were in the midst of some severe life crises. I had seen once before during my prior tour in Afghanistan, where a unit deployed a very troubled young man. Shortly after my arrival at Bagram AB this individual suffered a severe mental breakdown, threatened some female office workers with a knife and then went screaming off into our camp. With no jail or brig, no mental health personnel, no police force and with easy access to an assigned weapon, dealing with mentally unstable personnel was an extremely difficult problem in a combat location. In this case at Bagram, we disarmed the individual, had him evaluated by an Army doctor, which did not help us at all, and then had to assign him a 24/7 companion for the length of his remaining hours on base. One of our departing NCOs was taken from his assigned duties and given the task of watching this man, even when he went to the latrine, to prevent him from committing suicide attempt or further threatening other people. We sent him home within 12 hours with a watchdog companion for the journey to his home unit, until the responsibility was transferred to another NCO watcher midpoint in his flight. In that particular case, his home unit had sent him to the toughest combat assignment in the USAF despite the fact that he was already in treatment for aggression issues. He had also been found guilty of stalking a female co-worker. So, even with his prior serious discipline problems, his home unit in Hawaii had "dumped" him into the AEF system for several months with the ensuing drama and danger to other personnel at Bagram. He was later kicked out of the U.S. Air Force, mainly for this Bagram incident. So, I did have some experience with units sending us their problem personnel, however I never expected to see such a large number of cases or at such levels of dysfunction at Sather.

Every branch of the military is subject to Uniform Code of Military Justice (UCMJ) the same justice system. The UCMJ is different from US civil and criminal law. Its purpose is to maintain "good order and discipline". Good order and discipline is a concrete objective for all military units and their commanders. Minor disciplinary charges in a military unit can be handled using in order of severity, Counseling, a Letter of Counseling, a Letter of Reprimand and, finally, an Article 15. An Article 15 is non-judicial punishment and can gravely effect one's future military career. An Article 15 could cause one to lose rank and have pay reduced for a specific period. Above the Article 15 are the various levels of court martial, which are for more serious offenses. Since there were no courts martial in Iraq, I won't discuss them further. Suffice to stay that Article 15s are for minor offenses, but in the atmosphere of the 2006-7 active duty USAF they were almost certainly career-enders, once they returned to their unit. So, everyone, commanders and unit members, took Article 15s very seriously and they were the tool of last resort.

For a little perspective, in the ANG, our units had older and more mature people than the active duty units and consequently, our disciplinary problems were few and far between. I'd issued no Article 15s during my extended AEF tour at Bagram AB, Afghanistan (2002-3), nor did I issue any during 2-year stint as the wing commander of an ANG A-10 Wing in Pennsylvania. That would not be the case for the 447th AEG during my AEF tour.

The first personnel incident occurred in September, 2006, just after I had arrived from my Afghanistan detour. A 447th enlisted member arrived and we found that he had two Article 15s coming with him. One offense was committed in his home unit right before he left and the second Article 15 offense occurred in Qatar. Shortly after he was given his double Article 15 paperwork, he tried to commit suicide. He was within a minute or two from dying, from hanging, when he was luckily discovered by vigilant NCOs who were worried about his mental state. We sent him back to his unit in the U.S.

I could not believe that any competent unit commander would deploy a member who had a pending Article 15, with punishment to be served in Iraq. This was a gross example of a unit dumping its' worst people into Iraq and an example of remarkably poor leadership. When BG Rand heard about this he was justifiably furious and had me call the unit back in the United States about it. The colonel who I talked to initially was overly defiant - until I said that if I didn't get satisfaction, my boss, BG Rand, would be call *his* wing commander and inform him of this transgression. This was a gross abuse of the AEF system. This indiscretion would be the equivalent to a trucking company dumping its toxic waste into a National Park. After I made my threat to have the bosses talk the Group Commander Colonel went to an overly apologetic mode by saying (his exact wording), "What can I get for you [in Iraq]?" I wondered what he meant by that. I didn't take the bait because it implied something not allowed by GO1A (no booze, porn, etc.) and simply said, "Just send me a qualified and competent person to replace the one we sent back." Little did I know that three of our Article 15 personnel in Sather AB would come from this one single SF unit in the U.S. All of these people were sent over with severe discipline or personal issues, such as a nasty custody battle. In addition, they began their tour under the leadership of a negative, pissed off and ineffective leader, who wasn't interested in helping them solve their problems. No wonder they got into trouble.

We went through October with no personnel problems, but they were brewing. In early November, we had to issue and Article 15 to another SF Airman who had been mismanaging his finances. It also turned out that this individual had already received an Article 15 for financial malfeasance back at his home unit. He was from the very same unit as our suicide attempt individual, and whose Combat Support Group commander I had already called for sending us a person with an outstanding Article 15.

A couple days later, we caught two SF Airmen sleeping while on guard duty. This is a pretty serious offense because of the security problems that we were experiencing with BIAP. Our security forces were our first line of defense against a serious terrorist threat. Both individuals were given Article 15s for their carelessness. The continuing problems with our SF personnel (so far, all the Article 15s at Sather were for Security Forces people) were a direct result of the prior poor leadership and example of the fired SF commander. It was about this time that the new commander, LtCol Mezhir, arrived at Sather. He couldn't do anything about the prior discipline problems in his unit but quickly restored the morale and esprit de corps of his people.

In December, a bizarre case came to our attention. A female SF Airman told her supervisor a really unusual story. She said that her current boyfriend had told her that he had murdered someone while at home on leave. This was so serious that it had to be investigated. The boyfriend's home unit Office of Special Investigation (OSI) squadron looked into the case and found out that he had just made up the story of the alleged murder because the victim was still alive. However, her admission regarding her boyfriend created another problem since she had admitted to having sex in the women's tent, which was a violation of GO1A – no visiting the tent of the opposite sex. This resulted in a total of four individuals being issued Article 15s for this violation. The "boyfriend" in this case was, himself, in the middle of his second divorce and child custody case. He was from also from the same SF squadron that sent us two of our previous Article 15 cases, the ones involving the suicide attempt and the financial malfeasance. This one U.S. unit was obviously using the AEF system to send us their problem personnel. In another example of Wings sending personnel who were unqualified for a combat deployment, one of the females who received an Article 15 had been raped before her deployment by her husband, also a member of her SF unit. I was highly appalled by a unit deciding that it was appropriate to send a rape victim on a 6-month deployment to Iraq.

We experienced our last bit of personnel misconduct as we approached Christmas. An Airman attempted to destroy a vehicle by pouring sugar into the gas tank. When we asked him why he did it, he said that he just wanted to go home. He was duly awarded an Article 15 and, due to the seriousness of the case, we sent him to his home unit, where they decided to kick him out of the Air Force. We discovered later that he had a history at his home unit for stealing and financial problems.

After Christmas, I began to look at all the Article 15s issued at Sather and realized that over 50% were given to personnel that had either had discipline problems in their home unit, whether Article 15s or other discipline markers, or else they were going through a life crisis, such as a divorce and/or child custody battle. In addition, I discovered that all of the Article 15 level offenses were committed by people in the rank of E-5 or below.

Based on my examination, I devised a plan to ensure that these issues didn't happen again at Sather AB. This plan would apply to the next AEF tour following ours. We had every First Sergeant, the senior leadership NCO, in each squadron, interview each member below E-5 to see if they were going through a life crisis, such as a divorce / child custody battle or if they had ever received *any* disciplinary action from their home unit. Anyone falling into those two categories would receive special attention and counseling to keep them on the straight and narrow.

Also on December 31st I held a unit-wide commander's call. On that day, I talked to everyone in the unit. I addressed about 150-200 personnel in the main briefing room of the Glass House. The Glass House was the Sather headquarters building and had formerly been the VIP lounge for BIAP. I gave a 45-minute talk, which was a combination pep talk, along with warning about GO1A or other disciplinary mistakes. I gave five of these briefings, talking to everyone in the 447th AEG. I told everyone what a great job the unit had done over the last four months. We had started fast and kept the pace steady throughout the tour. However, it was now time to make sure we kept it all safe and secure until the end. By the way, there was no yelling or profanity in any of these talks.

The concept that I discussed had much to do with safety, but really applied to everything about our AEF tour. I called it the "beginning and end of tour message". The start and finish of the tours are the most dangerous periods, albeit for different reasons. In the beginning, everyone is learning the safest and most efficient way to do their job. They follow the rules and slowly get good at doing it efficiently. But during this early learning curve, accidents can happen. Conversely, at the end of the AEF tour, it also can be unsafe simply because everything has been going smoothly for months. That smoothness lulled people into a false sense of security and they begin to cut corners and not to follow the rules. That's why people are also in danger at the end of the tour.

So, I talked about the paradox of the beginning and ending of the tours and safety. But it wasn't just about safety that this theory of mine applied. It also had to do with security and discipline. The rules of GO1A still applied and it would be a tragedy to get an Article 15 just because one slipped up near the end of the tour. In fact, we had no further Article 15s after my Commander's Call that last day of the year.

Unfortunately for the 447th AEG and for me, there were a very small contingent of personnel that did not see receive my briefing on safety, security and discipline on the last day of 2006. These were members of the Explosive Ordnance Disposal (EOD) squadron, who were assigned to Army Forward Operating Bases (FOBs) outside of Baghdad. Had they received my briefing they might have been spared some casualties.

In summary, the vast majority of our assigned and volunteer personnel did a great job during their AEF tour. We celebrated each of their accomplishments in well attended and happy Iraqi Campaign Medal ceremonies in January, as people got ready to deploy home.

CHAPTER EIGHT
'BIAP IS BAD' BRIEFING

As the Air Force commander, responsible for the oversight of Baghdad International Airport (BIAP), I identified three major problems sets. First, were the security problems previously detailed in Chapter Six. Some of those issues we were able to handle surreptitiously, such as when we welded the tunnel access to the tower closed. Other problems took more time and cunning, as when we implemented an Iraqi ATC controller book, so we could get to know these workers and check their backgrounds, without their knowledge. The second set of problems dealt with the control and flow of air traffic into Sather Air Base (see Chapter 10). The third set of problems were those that dealt with the information I was getting from my Office of Special Investigation (OSI) unit concerning BIAP. Specifically, how BIAP was being used as a conduit for providing Iranian arms, money and fighters to the Shiite militias. What we didn't know was whether any of this material was being stored at BIAP. The subject of this chapter is this last set of problems at BIAP.

The initial discovery of the Iranian support flowing into BIAP came about during my predecessor's tour. However, he failed to tell anyone about it. So, it was up to me and my staff to act on the information. I began building a briefing about BIAP and the extra help I was going to need to search it for stored weapons, etc. For example, there was a village of houses in the northeast corner of the BIAP complex, where many of the BIAP workers lived. There were also all of the empty, derelict buildings across the runway from Sather Air Base. Were these buildings and areas being used to store weapons and materials for the anti-government forces? We didn't know. The 447th AEG had no access to these areas, since they were in Iraqi government territory, but I wanted to have them searched to make sure that they weren't being used as a weapons cache.

The number of weapons coming into Baghdad was alarming, with updated reports from my OSI team coming in almost every day. The OSI was focusing on BIAP, as I wanted, and providing me with solid evidence of the Iranian weapons coming in through the airport. After arrival, these weapons became invisible to us. Were they being stored at BIAP or traveling directly into Baghdad and possibly Sader City, a large slum district on the northeast side of Baghdad and a stronghold of the Jaish al-Mahdi (JAM), a Shiite militia group?

My first task was to let everyone know about the weapons, money and fighters flowing into the airport. I began to build a briefing based on the solid evidence provided by the numerous OSI reports that I was receiving, as well as my own observations and photographs.

My own photographs showed the JAM stickers on worker's lockers, the derelict buildings around BIAP that could be used as storage, the storage buildings that aroused so much attention when we went to inspect them. Finally, there was the actual weapons storage area with the hole in the fence and the weak protection around that important cache of Iraqi government ammunition.

With all this, I had a lot of ammunition for my briefing. In fact, as time passed, the briefing got bigger and more detailed as the reports of my OSI teams were updated. Even in the beginning, the briefing was hard hitting. I had no axe to grind and all of my OSI reports were new and accurate. By mid-October, my PowerPoint briefing was completed. I nicknamed it the "BIAP Is Bad" briefing. By late October 2006, I began the slow process of giving the briefing, starting with lower level State Department functionaries in the Green Zone (IZ or International Zone) in Baghdad. I was sponsored by the Iraq Reconstruction and Management Office (IRMO) shop at the State Department, so I began by briefing the leadership of that shop in late October.

The BIAP briefing was in three parts. The entire briefing was classified. Since I had *not* briefed my leadership at Balad AB, Iraq or the CENTAF Commanders at Al Udeid, Qatar I had to state that this briefing was my opinion wholly and not sanctioned by CENTAF. So, this was a Colonel Gregory Marston-only briefing. I had to use this disclaimer until I was able to give this briefing to Lt. General North on Christmas day. He then sanctioned this briefing and gave it immediate CENTAF approval at that time.

The second part of the briefing concerned the OSI reports on the influx of arms, money and fighters to the Shiite militias. It also included the pictures and the places that I had seen in BIAP myself. These included the empty, derelict buildings all over BIAP, the JAM stickers on worker's lockers, the almost non-existent security provided by the company guarding BIAP, and the weak security around the official Iraqi government weapons and ammunition storage area. It painted a bleak picture regarding BIAP, a facility which looked good on the outside but presented a potentially severe threat to us on the inside.

This part of the briefing also included a listing of all the initiatives that we had taken at Sather to negate potential threats from BIAP. These included: the construction of the Sather "fortress" by the addition of 1500 12' tall, Alaskan blast barriers and 100 bomb shelters; the four Readiness Exercises that we had conducted at Sather to prepare ourselves from any BIAP attacks (with pictures included in the briefing) and the movement of the Fire Department and EOD from their old clubhouse 300 yards from the BIAP perimeter to a safer position on Sather- proper over 1000 yards away. The point of this part of the briefing was that the 447th AEG took this threat very seriously and had done everything within our power at Sather AB to address it.

The last section was a "way ahead" for addressing the potential threat posed by the condition of BIAP. What I wanted was to have the Army provide a unit to search each house in the BIAP village for cached weapons and then to do the same for the empty buildings around BIAP. I could augment this Army unit with my Security Forces (SF) personnel, but we didn't have enough people to do it by ourselves. This action portion of the briefing was my own creation and had never been done in the three and a half years since the Americans had set up operations at Sather AB. With the "do nothing" attitude of the Army hierarchy in Iraq, I knew that there would be pushback on this part of the briefing, but I also felt that we had to take this action to clean out BIAP if there were weapons stored there. Those potential weapons and ammo were a danger not only to us but to the entire Victory Base Complex.

I began by giving my first briefing to the IRMO hierarchy in the Green Zone. Then I began to work my way up the State Department and military pecking order in the Green Zone. I began to notice an interesting phenomenon as I worked my way up the food chain in the International Zone. As long as I was willing to be the one to present this briefing, which could be shot down at any time, other functionaries would keep pushing me higher up the ranks of the civilian and military channels. These supporters wanted me to succeed, but by having me give the briefing, instead of them, all the risk fell upon me if there was ever disapproval toward the briefing. I didn't care because I was on a mission to make BIAP and Sather safer and my OSI sources were unbiased and presenting credible intelligence.

In addition to my bi-weekly trips to the Green Zone to give this briefing, I found other venues of my own for preaching the message. I had learned the way the Army operates after working with them very closely in Bagram AB, Afghanistan. One lesson from that tight relationship in Afghanistan was the power of the Command Sergeant Majors in the Army. These are the highest ranking enlisted NCOs (E-9s) in that service. These senior NCOs worked closely with the colonels and general officers in the Army. So, if you wanted to talk to a general then speak to the Command Sergeant Majors first and it would be relayed through them! So, in early November, I briefed the 54 Command Sgt. Majors of VBC on my Baghdad briefing. They received it warmly and the word was spread: BIAP was a problem and the Air Force at Sather was serious about doing something about it.

Another audience that I targeted in October was the VBC Base Commanders Board. This was a group of colonels, all Army except for me, that dealt with the various problems of the VBC. In my first visit to this board, I delivered my briefing. This was how I approached the Army – always stay on the offensive. My briefing to the Base Commanders Board caught them by surprise and also established my legitimacy with this group. So, whenever I needed something from this group, I could now get their support, because they viewed me as a serious player. In fact, when I needed to help the Iraqis to expand the New Al Muthana base property so they could spread out their newly acquired Soviet Mi-8 helicopters, I just made the call to the Base Commanders Board and they responded, having the Iraqis take over ramp space from another Army unit, the VBC Post Office. The Iraqis needed the extra ramp space to increase the spacing between their helicopters due to the rocket attacks, so I was glad to help them. As I said before, always stay on the offensive with the Army.

In mid-November, I briefed the deputy CENTAF commander, MG Holland, on the BIAP issues. As a result of this briefing, he gave me the task of moving the Fire Department and EOD onto the Sather property.By late November, I was briefing higher levels of the State Department ranks in the Green Zone. Most of the reaction I got was one of surprise from the State Department wonks. No one had taken the time or effort to articulate the problems at BIAP and how it was negatively impacting the entire Iraq War, which in my opinion, we were losing.

Finally, in early December, I went to the Green Zone to brief the US Ambassador to Iraq, Ambassador Joseph Saloom. I entered the room to deliver my briefing to about ten State Department executives and one Navy Rear Admiral. They introduced me to the group but I did not know who they were except for the Ambassador. I put a great deal of effort into this briefing because I was addressing the highest echelon of the State Department in Iraq. By this time, I had given this briefing about a dozen times. Furthermore, I had continued to update it with 447th OSI reports so it was a robust, fact-filled report. As I gave this briefing I could feel the shock and surprise of the State Department functionaries. Up until this briefing, I believe that no one had given them this sort of damning evidence about the potential threat from BIAP. As I continued, I began to feel that I might have actually reached my goal and get what I needed in the third part of my brief, which was a list of proposed actions to be taken. I felt like the dog who had just caught the car it had been chasing for months. When I reached the end of my briefing, I was asked the "how do we fix this" question. I again reiterated my request for Army soldiers to augment Sather SF personnel to search and clean out BIAP. That, plus implementing more stringent arrival procedures there. Everyone seemed amenable to this course of action.

It was then that Ambassador Saloom asked the Rear Admiral, the only military member of the panel, what he thought. This naval officer narrowed his gaze and then pointed his finger to me and said, "Marston, your plan has not been vetted". As soon as he said this, it was as if all the air suddenly leaked out of the balloon I had blown up with this briefing. What the Admiral was saying was that my plan would have to go through the "do nothing" layers of military bureaucracy, with the end result being that nothing would change. The risk aversion part of the military hierarchy had won. I was crushed.

I returned to Sather in a funk. I had been so close to getting what I needed for BIAP. I felt like all of my briefings had been for naught. But this was not the end of the tale. For a week of two, I thought I had hit the end of the trail. I continued to give the BIAP briefing to whoever would listen.

On Christmas Day, I was able to deliver this briefing to LtGen North, the CENTAF Commander. He was convinced of the threat and made this a CENTAF-sanctioned briefing. I had Special Agent Kristy Wheeler, the commander of the OSI unit, brief about the intelligence that they had collected concerning the terrorists use of BIAP. She gave a masterful presentation that was well received by North.

Two weeks after I gave the briefing to the Ambassador I had a visitor to the Glass House VIP lounge, right next to my office. It was the same Rear Admiral who had shot down my plan in the Green Zone. He was on his way home to the States so I wasn't that shocked, because I was used to the "risk aversion bubble" from the general officers in Iraq. I was civil to him, but I made the point of saying that we're still here at Sather and that nothing had changed at BIAP. It went right over his head. He had saved himself from having to vet my plan during the last days of his tour. Personally, I wanted to kick him in the ass, but I was just a colonel in charge of a base, so I steamed in private as he went home. Due to him, nothing had changed.

Late in December, the VBC Defensive Force got a new commander. He was an Iowa Army National Guard colonel. I viewed this as an opportunity and went to see him to give him the BIAP briefing. At the end of the briefing he said to me, "You're the first person to tell me anything about what's going on around here". I was happy to find someone of a kindred spirit, who was in a position to actually do something for me at Sather! We talked and worked out a plan for addressing the threats to Sather and VBC, which wouldn't require any vetting from the higher ups. We decided to begin the cleanup of BIAP by having his VBC defense force work together with our Sather AB SF personnel.

In early January, we put this plan into motion. We went into the BIAP village and began to search the houses for weapons and ammunition caches. We expected the village towns people to oppose our searches, but, instead, we got quite the opposite reaction. They wanted us to find any anti-government caches. Much like a town with a good sheriff, the BIAP people wanted to be safe and we were the only ones who were in a position to make that happen. Ultimately, we did not find anything of significance in our searches. But we now knew that the BIAP village was safe.

I left Iraq before the investigation of the derelict buildings in BIAP occurred. But the point was that it did occur and that is the most important element. We each add our bricks toward the proverbial "building of a house" so that it is always getting better and better.

I must admit, ten years later, that I did not have a predetermined list of people to whom I wanted to present this briefing. Initially, I was concerned with building the most persuasive and accurate presentation that I could make, then giving it to anyone who would listen. So, the list of my recipients was largely ad hoc over the three-month period in which I gave this briefing. I had two target audiences which I intended to pursue simultaneously: the first was the State Department leadership, whose chain I was determined to brief as far as possible, sounding the alarm regarding the influx of incoming Iranian weapons, money and material into BIAP. That audience was important but probably couldn't assist me in my quest to search BIAP for nefarious storage areas. The second audience was my Army peers from the VBC, looking for their help in performing searches into areas on BIAP where weapons caches or gun firing positions might be located. I probably should have given BG Rand this presentation, but there never really was a good time to do that. At the same time, he would have been unable to help me with Army assistance into BIAP; nor could he order me to move the EOD squadron, as Maj Gen Holland did; nor could he give me the CENTAF "certificate of approval" that only LtGen North could and eventually did give on Christmas Day, 2006.

In summary, I briefed everyone that I could about the incursion of Iranian weapons, ammunition, money and personnel into BIAP. As a mere colonel in Iraq, I was able to light that torch all the way up to the Ambassador level in the State Department. Although initially thwarted on my plan to clean out BIAP by the bureaucrats, I was finally able to do so at my level of command. I just kept carrying the message until it resonated with someone who also recognized the risk there.

Strategically, I also think that my messages on BIAP's problems and the overall effect of the Iranian influx of weapons slightly influenced the war in Iraq. Only when military leaders tell the truth can the civilian hierarchy make the decisions necessary to win the war. I raised the flag of dangerous activities concerning BIAP and Iran. This certainly was a real shock to the audience at the Ambassador level. This would have made them more pliable toward other briefings on the dangers in Iraq. It is worth noting that the Surge, Gen Petraeus's massive influx of troops in Iraq, happened only five months after I gave my BIAP brief at the highest level in Iraq. I'd like to believe that my briefing was a very small step forward and perhaps helped *light the path* toward the Surge's start. So, the hidden benefit from my briefing may have had far more of an effect than the mere tactical victory that I had scored. I do particularly remember an Army military officer telling me heatedly after hearing my briefing: "Colonel Marston, we [the U.S. military] will *NEVER* enter Sader City". That event happened during the Surge, which began only a few months after my last briefing and subsequent deal with the VBC Defense Commander.

CHAPTER NINE
SAFEST BASE IN IRAQ

Although Sather Air Base was facing the weak security arrangement of BIAP and its empty, derelict buildings and we had an occasional rocket shelling, we worked through training of our people and construction to build the safest base in Iraq. I previously detailed in Chapter 6 the security problems of Sather and how we addressed those issues. This chapter will discuss the other steps which I took to further the safety of the men and women of Sather, on and off the base.

Besides the building of Sather into a robust fortress with our 1500 12' Alaskan barriers and over 100 bomb shelters, I worked hard to create a feeling at Sather of it being a safe and secure base. We talked about it often because we had the safest base on VBC. Even though we had eight persons per tent, with all their possessions in unlocked trunks, we had no theft at the base. Meanwhile, VBC was having a veritable crime wave on their side of the complex. I know this because I had CMSgt Gordon Swarthout brief everyone, during our weekly staff meetings, of the crime occurring in VBC. This criminal activity ranged from theft, assaults and then graduated to much more serious crimes like sexual assault. The policing of VBC was almost impossible. First, there were over 60,000 Army troops there with seeming little to do, because of the risk aversion decision-making cloud hanging over the hierarchy then. Next there were the tens of thousands of contractor civilians in VBC who were not under General Order 1A (no alcohol, etc.). These contractor camps were scattered all over VBC and had no policing or military supervision. Although most ran a clean ship, there were rumors of criminal activities (like prostitution) at some of them. Contractors were generally older, and mostly prior military, so I think that they were generally on board with winning the war. Yet, they were also under less supervision than the average soldier, during their off-duty hours. It didn't matter who was committing the crime outside of Sather on VBC. We couldn't let it enter Sather and I had to figure out how to protect our airmen when they left the base.

I decided the handle the problems of the airmen going to VBC, and being preyed upon, in two ways. First, I issued a new order that specified that our airmen must be armed at all times when outside Sather. That showed our people how serious the issues were outside the comparative safety of Sather.

Also, except for EOD personnel on missions or myself, or my staff, on the way to Balad AB or the Green Zone, *no one* was able to go outside of VBC. This order was part of the Vietnam era solution to the problem of troops wandered around Saigon or the countryside in search of entertainment, fun or adventure. Here people were restricted to a much safer environment as it was on VBC.

VBC offered the chance to try other dining halls. You could tour the various palaces of VBC and to visit the several Base Exchanges (BX) in that area. It was ok to visit these different areas of VBC but what I didn't want was our airmen to feel that they could take lonely strolls or runs through the base complexes there in the evening or night.

The second part of my new security order had to do with visiting VBC by solo airmen. It started with our own little BX complex on Sather. Besides a little trailer-sized BX we had several other rooms with different activities such as men's and women's haircuts. All the hair cutters were Moslem contract workers and all were men. I never had any problem with them, although after I had a very short haircut (for $3), I opted out of the complimentary shoulder and head massage. Just not my style. However, while getting a haircut in the Sather BX area, a solo woman airman was touched in an inappropriate place by one of the male hair cutters in the women's salon. I was furious and wanted to bring the offending male contractor under the uniform Code of Military Justice. Unfortunately, that was not how the system worked there. This contractor was simply sent home. Nothing was changed in the operation of these little shops because they were just part of a bigger operation.

This was a big problem with the contractor services in Iraq. The companies there hired Moslems anywhere but from Iraq. We could have made friends and allies of local Iraqis who would then have been invested in the reconstruction process. Instead we *imported* Moslems, who all had to be screened by USAF security anyway, before they entered Sather for work every single day.

I met with the head contractor general in the USAF late in my tour, and *only then* were they realizing something that was obvious to me from day one – that we needed to hire local Iraqis into the low-end contractor jobs on the bases. So, for three and a half years Iraqis were kept out of hundreds if not thousands of menial contractor jobs *in Iraq*! Once again, history was being ignored. America had used base jobs to give locals work after the wars in Germany, Japan, Korea and Afghanistan. But not in Iraq. I had tried to fight this system almost immediately upon arrival into Sather.

In the first days of my tour, I was approached by the owner of a small Iraqi gift shop and uniform pressing operation on Sather. He said that 12 Iraqi families depended on these two operations. They were scheduled to be closed and replaced by a big American company, who would use foreign Moslem laborers. Twice I went to bat for this little shop with the leadership in VBC. Twice I was told that there was "nothing to be done" about it. I couldn't save that little Iraqi shop nor change the policies of the BX haircut people. So, I approached the problem from another angle.

I added another rule for all the airmen at Sather - anyone who used the haircut places there had to go into the shops with at least one other person. The force of numbers would keep everyone safe from the Moslem workers. I also extended the two-person policy in our Sather BX area to the entire VBC area. No one from the 447th AEG could go into VBC without being part of a two-person group or more as well as being armed. After the haircut incident, no one else was hurt, robbed or molested from Sather AB for the rest of our AEF tour.

I analyzed all of the old Operating Instructions (OIs) for Sather AB. Operating Instructions are the local amendments to the basic military regulations and there were about a dozen of them on file at Sather. All were outdated and were not even publicized anymore. So, I canceled them all and in their place instituted a single Operating Instruction concerning the two-person and firearm rules for members of the 447th AEG. To go onto VBC you needed to carry your firearm and go in two-person or more teams.

The other rule that we kept and perpetuated was the tight and limited access to Sather living areas. Only those who lived there or had a one-day layover (Air Force convoy drivers or flight aircrew) were given a pass card to gain entry to the Sather living town. You had to work on Sather to live there. This contrasted with the Army living areas which were open to all military and civilian traffic in VBC. By limiting access to only those who lived at Sather we kept the living area safe and had no crime of any kind in that area. Sather became the safest base in VBC by strict access, protecting our airmen in VBC and the training of our people for the rocket attacks that plagued our base and the other camps.

CHAPTER TEN
REDESIGNING THE DANGEROUS TRAFFIC FLOW INTO BIAP AND OTHER AIR TRAFFIC SAFETY PROBLEMS

During my base-wide tour of Sather, I eventually visited the 10-story high BIAP Air Traffic Control tower, which was located in the Iraq-controlled part of the airfield. Besides being appalled by the numerous and severe security problems, I was also stunned by the significant air traffic control issues. BIAP and Sather had been a joint use civilian and military operation of a two-runway system for over three years and, as with other issues, I assumed that it would be a smoothly-running machine by this time. It was not. Again, I fell back on my extensive experience as a Supervisor of Flying (SOF) at my A-10 squadron in Pennsylvania, as the American SOF and pilot liaison while working in the Kuwaiti control tower at Al Jaber Air Base in Kuwait and during my numerous interactions with the Bagram Air Base tower in Afghanistan. I would need all of my experience to solve the protracted problems of the BIAP/Sather ATC issues.

One of the first questions regarding the BIAP tower was what provisions existed in case the tower lost electrical power or their radios? There was no backup of any kind – not in another facility or even spare radios! Even the dumpy and rundown Bagram AB, Afghanistan control tower had a backup operation in 2002. Yet, the multi-million dollar BIAP tower had nothing in reserve. Considering the jury-rigged nature of the electrical system, basically a generator with cables bypassing the derelict electronics of the tower - this was an accident waiting to happen.

The BIAP tower had no backup radios of any kind nor was an alternate facility for running air operations if something bad would happen, whether by accident (smoke or fire) or by attack (direct assault or kidnapping of our personnel). I viewed this as an inexcusable oversight by all of the previous commanders at Sather. There was no "Plan B" in case of any emergency in the BIAP tower. Considering the high number of American troops transitioning thru Sather every day, this deficiency had to be dealt with immediately.

We ordered backup radios for the tower and shopped around for an alternative tower operation. At Bagram, we had imported a mini-tower trailer to fill this need and exercised it occasionally to make sure it was ready to go, in case it was needed.

When MG Holland, the deputy CENTAF Commander, came for his first visit I specifically asked for expeditious help in getting the equipment we needed. I think he was slightly surprised because, usually, when the general asks if you "need any help" everyone routinely defers on this request. However, I felt that our deficiencies at Sather were so great that being diplomatic was not an option - we needed help now! He was able to very quickly get us a couple of backup radios for the tower, and that filled our immediate need.

The backup tower operation took a little more time. Eventually we were able to procure a fully operational Humvee with a full complement of Very High Frequency (VHF) and Ultra-High Frequency (UHF) radios to be used as spares in case the BIAP tower was incapacitated, either by enemy action or by accident. We kept the backup radio Humvee at Sather, for safe keeping, after certifying that all of the radios in it worked and were ready for an emergency.

The physical issues of the BIAP tower were the easiest to solve. The operational issues of the air traffic control system were going to take some work. Here is how a normal tower and aircraft interface works, so you can see how safety and lookout are maximized. Then I'll show you how the dangerous and restricted operation at BIAP was just an "accident waiting to happen" in late 2006.

In a normal air traffic control tower operation, it is critical to maximize the number of eyes looking outside the windows of the tower and aircraft to make sure that accidents and near-misses are minimized. Tower crews have three and sometimes four major tasks. They control ground operations, depending on the size of the airport, they may issue flight clearances, they monitor aircraft operating in their control zone and they coordinate the approach/departure areas to control arriving and departing aircraft. Nothing taxis, takes off, lands or operates in their control zone without their clearance. The tower personnel watch all aircraft moving on the ground and in the air within their control area.

Simultaneously, all aircrews operating in this tower control zone are constantly looking outside to ensure that no conflicts arise between themselves and other aircraft as they approach or depart from the field. In addition to all of these people performing visual lookout, there are mandatory radio calls which pilots make to let controllers know where they are in the airport. When a pilot says, "Holding short" this tells everyone on this radio frequency that they are holding off the runway on the taxiway and are ready for takeoff. The radio call of "Position and hold" indicates that an aircraft has been cleared to taxi out onto the runway and will hold for takeoff clearance. "Cleared for takeoff" means you are now cleared for takeoff down the runway. These radio calls are issued by the tower and repeated back by the aircraft pilots so everyone on the radio channel can build a *mental picture* of what other aircraft are doing in the runway/airport environment, in addition to what they can see outside their aircraft or tower windows.

That is a normal air traffic control operation. However, what we had a BIAP / Sather Air Base was drastically different and much more dangerous. First, they had one set of radios set up for fixed wing (normal aircraft) on both runways and another set of radios set up for the helicopters that were flying around Sather. With the limited aircraft traffic at BIAP / Sather, about a hundred-total aircraft takeoff and landings a day, fixed wing aircraft de-confliction was not a problem. The real danger was de-confliction between the helicopter and aircraft traffic. Because the helicopter traffic was on a separate frequency from the fixed-wing aircraft traffic, neither could get that mental picture of where everyone was inside the airfield control zone because they were unable to *hear* or communicate with each other.

The second problem with the de-confliction (i.e., avoiding each other) program at Sather was that the aircraft / helicopters could not always *see* each other either because of different fixed wing/rotary wing external lighting policies for operations during the hours of darkness. In normal military/civilian operations, all aircraft display their external lights for maximum visibility at all times. When I arrived at Sather, aircraft were arriving/departing with wildly differing levels of external lighting. Many kept their lights off all the way until landing because they were worried about taking fire from Baghdad, while they were on the long, non-maneuvering final approach at Sather. So, there was no coherent set of rules at Sather Air Base for aircraft lighting. Helicopters and aircraft were mostly keeping their lights off at night. All of this would have been okay if Sather had been a night vision goggles (NVG)-only airfield as had been the case when I was at Bagram Air Base in 2002-3. Unfortunately, we were not at that point, far from it. The dangerous flaw at Sather Air Base, with so many aircraft operating with their lights off, was that many of the pilots, and more importantly, the ATC staff in the tower, were NOT wearing NVGs. So, we had aircraft arriving and departing at night whose pilots were not wearing NVGs and with their external lights off.

When I was at Bagram AB, Afghanistan from 2002-3 we operated a totally blacked out, NVG-only airfield. *It was the only airfield like it in the world.* It was a very intense arrangement. Everything on the air base, as well as the army base had to be set up for this type of operation. During the hours of darkness, anyone driving a vehicle of any kind on the base, had to be wearing NVGs. Pilots, cargo loaders, anyone driving on the airfield taxiways, the air traffic controllers in the tower and truck drivers on the base itself were all wearing NVGs. The entire base operated in complete black out condition. No lights were on anywhere on the base. For instance, as you walked around in the dark on sidewalks, next to you were large trucks on the road with all their lights off. You couldn't see the trucks, you just heard them. Aircraft came in for landings with lighting that could only be seen through NVGs. To the naked eye, they were completely dark. Everyone on the airfield and roads drove around with their lights off. All the tents and buildings near the runway were configured for a blacked-out operation like they had in WWII cities. All windows were closed and covered over so that no light inside would leak out. The actual lighting on the airfield itself was special infrared (IR) lighting visible only using NVGs. Bagram was configured and operated like this every single night during my tour and there were no accidents related to the blacked-out operation. But the blacked-out base worked at Bagram because everyone participated and knew the problems associated with it from the start. It was an extremely intense and dangerous wartime operation.

Sather was operating on a partially blacked-out manner, with external lighting based on the decisions of the pilots and not on a comprehensive airbase policy. The only pilots that used NVGs at Sather on a constant basis were the Army helicopter pilots. In fact, the helicopter pilots were the sole participants in the airfield operation that had a reasonable chance of using "see and avoid" procedures. With the ATC controllers and many of the cargo aircraft pilots not under NVGs, they were unable to see other fixed wing aircraft or helicopters, that almost always had their external lights turned off. It was unsafe and needed to be changed.

Finally, Sather lacked established helicopter arrival/departure routes around the airfield. Normally, airports have established navigation routes with named waypoints based on geographical features. Using this method, a helicopter can call a waypoint name as they pass over it and everyone on the radio frequency would know their position. When I arrived at Sather, helicopters were choosing their own routing over the airfield and since they were blacked-out, it was solely up to them to avoid arriving and departing cargo aircraft. Unfortunately, they were often flying right underneath cargo aircraft on final approach for landing. In one dangerous incident, a cargo aircraft experienced a Terminal Collision Avoidance System (TCAS) anti-collision alarm when it was only 300' above ground level while preparing to land. Upon investigation, we discovered that a helicopter had flown *underneath* the aircraft which was less than a minute from landing. That incident enlightened us that the current system was deeply flawed because no one had seen the helicopter as it passed under the aircraft on final approach. The only way we knew it happened was because of the TCAS alarm.

So, it became clear that Sather had a disjointed, dangerous and unsound ATC system. We were going to have to transition Sather to either a totally blacked out, all NVG arrangement, like at Bagram or a to a completely lighted and conventional operation like that at every military airbase. There was no option for something in the middle. We had to overcome the challenges of having aircraft and helicopters on different radio frequencies with neither being able to hear the other, of having pilots determining their own lighting procedures over the airfield and finally of having helicopters choose their own routing to keep them away from enemy anti-aircraft fire, but putting them near the path of aircraft landing or departing. The current unsafe mode of operation had been in place for three and a half years. Fortunately, no one had died in a mid-air collision... yet, but it was a system ripe for disaster.

The fixes to this operation were going to have to be implemented systematically because most of the pilots flying into Sather were not stationed here. First, we needed to design a safe arrival/departure route for the helicopters that would keep them away from ground anti-aircraft fire, as well as separated from the departing/landing aircraft and finally flying over reporting points so everyone knew where they were. Fortunately, we had some British helicopters stationed at Sather, so I conferred with them about ground tracks would keep the helos away from the areas where they were likely to encounter anti-aircraft fire, yet also de-conflicted them from the departure and approach corridors of the fixed wing aircraft. We located points of reference on the ground, such as prominent hills, road intersections or buildings that they could easily see as they flew the route. We named each of the major points on the routes so that when they called out each point on the radio, everyone from the aircraft pilots to the air traffic controllers would know where they were, all working to create a mental picture of their flight path. Since I was designing this helicopter routing I decided to name each of these reporting points after the A-10 aircraft, which was nicknamed the Warthog. Each point had to be five letters so they had names like BACON or HHOGG. The new helicopter routing solved three separate problems. It de-conflicted the helicopters from the aircraft departing or landing by the use of mandatory radio calls over known reference points. It standardized the routing so that that helicopters knew where to fly, using actual ground reference points, along with Global Positioning System (GPS) coordinates, if so equipped. Finally, it kept the helicopters inside the VBC boundaries, so that they were safe from enemy ground fire from Baghdad.

The next part of the safety program was to get everyone on the same radio frequency so that aircraft and helicopters arriving and departing from Sather would finally be able to hear each other. By having all aircraft and helicopters call out their respective reporting points both sets of pilots could visualize where the others were, even if they couldn't see them.

The last part of the de-confliction system was to have everyone turn on their external lights as they approached the field. They could keep their lights off while over Baghdad to avoid making them vulnerable, however, as they approached Sather, they all had to turn all of their lights on.

Once we had designed the helicopter/aircraft de-confliction system, we needed to publicize it. Fortunately, the Army was sponsoring a helicopter safety conference in October, 2006 at VBC. This was attended by most, if not all, of the helicopter operators in this part of Iraq. I obtained a place on the conference agenda to deliver a presentation about the current de-confliction nightmare at Sather and our plan to fix it. Of course, I briefed it before putting it into effect. I initially received some pushback from the rotary wing leadership until they realized that we had selected helicopter reporting points with actual ground references which had been vetted by the British helicopter pilots. They also appreciated that we kept them well inside the VBC boundaries and away from any ground fire. Finally, they understood that everyone would be on the same radio frequency and that their lights would be turned on. The Army now understood about our new anti-collision program. The Air Force pilots would also have to be informed. I sent Lt Col Chris Finter, the only other pilot on the 447th AEG staff and the commander of the Operations Squadron, south down to Ali Air Base to brief the C-130 pilots on our program. He did an excellent job and we received positive feedback on his presentation there. The rest of the Air Force pilots would have to read about our new system via the Notice to Airmen (NOTAM) system, in which we explained the hazards to the current program, such as helicopters on the aircraft flight path and our new plan to fix it.

Once we designed the new plan it was finally time to implement it. This entire project took almost two months to implement. I was nervous on the first day, but excited that we were finally fixing this dangerous issue. The immediate feedback we received was that aircraft pilots finally realized that helicopters were near them as they came into land. They knew this now because everyone was now on the same radio frequency. Most were *shocked* by this realization, because they couldn't hear or see them before. Now we had a fully functional anti-collision and de-confliction program at Sather. Once we got past the first couple of days of the new system, I was ecstatic because now we had a functioning system to keep all the thousands of troops flying into and out of Sather safe.

This is another example of a serious problem at Sather that had been "kicked down road" by previous commanders. I suspect that few, if any, knew of this problem. Only with a commander's involvement could a problem of this magnitude be solved. Only by asking questions in the control tower was it exposed to me. It had been an "accident waiting to happen" for years and only by the grace of God had nothing occurred previously in terms of a fatal mid-air collision possibly involving hundreds of troops.

It demonstrates that big problems can be solved if you keep applying pressure to them over time. Lt Col Finter did much of the leg work in this critical project and we didn't shirk from the time or effort required to resolve this issue. Sometimes you just have to think and act big. This particular problem took almost two months to resolve, from designing a remedy, to drawing the charts for the approach plates and maps, writing the NOTAMS and then briefing as many participants as possible. This was another example of a major vulnerability at Sather Air Base solved as quickly as possible, which would benefit the future AEF rotations.

CHAPTER ELEVEN
MORALE BOOSTERS

The main goal for the 447th AEG was to do our mission well and to contribute to the war effort. We succeeded in our combat role in Iraq. The 447th AEG set many records during our tour, including year-long records for numbers of passengers and amounts of cargo moved. We were the biggest mover of passengers and the second largest movers of cargo transferred within Iraq. We set an all-time Sather Air Base record for aviation fuel pumped. In perspective, Sather Air Base was moving *five times the passengers and cargo* handled by Ramstein Air Force Base, Germany or Al Udeid, Qatar even though these huge bases had ten times the number of personnel. Even with far less personnel and our crude outdoor facilities we achieved a high level of performance. This was the power of creating a warrior ethos and great morale for our people.

This amazing mission orientation had been helped immeasurably by excellent morale and a belief in our objectives. Yet, I had been in previous air wings where the wing commander achieved the mission goals simply by beating everyone into submission. That was not my plan at Sather and I wanted to keep morale as high as possible while completing the mission. So, we considered it very important to do anything possible toward raising the self-confidence and the spirits of the 447th airmen. We started early by training of all personnel in the combat first aid (SABC – Self-Aid and Buddy Care) and the Operational Readiness Exercises. I also felt that the 1.5 mile run/walk in body armor, while not fun on the surface, would show our personnel what they could actually do while wearing the 65 pounds of armor protection. On the six days during our tour that we actually wore body armor at Sather, our people performed well in that gear. It was all about showing everyone that they are capable of doing far more than they thought – greatly improving everyone's self-confidence.

We modified a program used in the USAF, called the "shiny penny". In the regular Air Force when a general or civilian VIP comes to visit, he/she will meet a select few deserving airmen to shake their hand and perhaps to give out a few challenge coins.

Challenge coins were carried by almost all military generals and even a few civilians. The higher the rank or command of the generals the more elaborate the coins would be. As I stated earlier, they were highly sought after by all personnel. Challenge coins were all the rage in the Global War on Terrorism. For the average airmen in an active duty USAF wing, they might expect to receive a coin for superior work from their squadron commander, usually a Major or Lt Colonel. Here at Sather, we could vastly increase this ante.

I would often get calls from a general's staff who wanted to arrange a visit to Sather. I would *always* ask the command staff if the general would like to shake some hands and give out some challenge coins. They in turn, *always* wanted to do that. We would negotiate to try to get as many challenge coins, given by the general, as possible. From there we would send out messages to all squadrons at Sather looking for "shiny penny" candidates, personnel who were doing exceptional work, especially if they had not been "coined" before. We'd get one person from each squadron. We'd group all these superstars together for the general to meet. The best of the best would get the challenge coins, the rest a handshake. So, we used the deluge of brass visiting Sather to reward our people. It was a big motivator for people to excel in their Sather job, to get a once in a lifetime chance to "get coined" at Sather by a high-ranking officer. Literally we got several hundred personnel "coined" at Sather with this method.

We used the same approach for politicians visiting Sather. We would typically make an announcement over the base loudspeakers for "Anyone from Pennsylvania or New Hampshire (or whatever state the politicians were from) please come to the Glass House" (the 447th unit headquarters). We never said who would be at the Glass House, for security reasons, but our people got the message. The politicians got to meet their constituents and the airmen got to meet their Senators or Congressmen. We'd tell our Airmen that, "our mission is so important, which is why we were visited so often". This was a big morale boost for all our people. The "shiny penny" and politician visits were easy and painless ways of raising morale at Sather. We milked that cow for all it was worth and got people working very hard to "get coined" in the bargain.

With Sather being the gateway into Iraq, we had many famous people visit the base. We always tried to use this to our advantage. For instance, Secretary of Defense Rumsfeld came to visit us twice during his tenure and we used these stopovers to reward our star performers. On his last visit to Iraq, before he was fired, we had twelve star performers in the 447th there to greet him. As he made his way through the handshakes, an energetic member of my staff, Senior Airman (SrA) "Robo" Brabham gave him one of our unit's Christmas cards. That card got Brabham a signed letter of appreciation from Secretary Rumsfeld.

The Christmas card was my creation and was sent out to every member of our command electronically. It was entitled "Season's Greetings from Baghdad" and had a picture of the young members of the Sather honor guard in formation in front of the Glass House on the cover. Another beautiful picture of State Street was on the inside page. I wrote a mission message on the inside about what we were doing at Sather Air Base. It informed people that we were a USAF combat unit made up of Active Duty, Air Force Reserve and Air National Guard members. I said that morale was high as we contributed to the Global War on Terrorism. It concluded by saying, "We fight for you and our great nation. Airpower!" It included the names of all the commanders at Sather. I was pretty proud of this creation and encouraged members to send it home electronically. We gave out paper copies to visitors in the holiday season.

Besides Rumsfeld we also had cordial visits from Senator Clinton, Senator Kerry, Senator McCain and Senator Lieberman, among others. Senator McCain, as a former prisoner of war (POW) was a big favorite among the airmen. I conversed with the Senator and said that I had flown with his son, Doug, at American Airlines. I spent the most time talking to Senator Lieberman from Connecticut while McCain was being mobbed by our airmen. Lieberman was a down to earth guy and asked me straightforwardly how the war was really going. The question caught me by surprise and to my shame, I gave a bland answer, because I was worried that if I told the truth it might impact my promotion. I regret that. Of all the politicians, I was most impressed with Lieberman and McCain and least impressed by John Kerry, who seemed in a daze during his visit.

Still, I thanked both Kerry and McCain for their combat service to our nation.

Another visitor was Secretary of State Condoleezza Rice, whose arrival I had to delay for security reasons. I shook her hand and had a minute or two to talk with her. She was also a nice person and was well updated on the Iraq War. But for all the political superstars we had feted at Sather, it was the pop stars that really stirred our airmen's interest.

Approaching the holiday season, we had a visit by the World Wrestling Entertainment (WWE). We did not get the most famous stars from that organization but still got some patriotic wrestlers who were good enough to volunteer to come to Iraq over the holidays. The Army gave us a few hours with them and we used it to full advantage. We brought them to the Glass House for a filmed advertisement, some pictures and then to hang out with the airmen. Hundreds came to see their heroes. I honestly thought that the WWE was stupid and not a real sport. I didn't really want to have anything to do with the wrestlers. But I went anyway and was really surprised. First of all, I was shocked with how many airmen showed up to see them – hundreds from our Group. Secondly, I was impressed with the wrestlers themselves – they were all fit, smart, funny and excellent communicators. They had volunteered to come to Iraq and Afghanistan and that meant a lot to us. We had a lot of fun with them. I gave them each a 447th AEG challenge coin and a bunch of us went under the mirrored dome of the Glass House to scream "Airpower, Airpower!" in front of the cameras. They were great. They even had time to sign the State Street wall and to visit our wounded in the base hospital. I worried that one of our wounded airmen, hurt in a rocket attack, would pull out his drip lines because he got so excited that the WWE had come to visit him.

The most impressive visitor to Iraq, in my opinion, was the singer, Kid Rock. He came on Christmas day and once again was mobbed by a crowd of hundreds of airmen. He was a really nice guy and went out of his way to sign autographs and take pictures. I told the packed Glass House, "This man [Kid Rock] lives a life that we can only imagine, yet he has sacrificed to come here to visit us on this holiday. It shows how important our mission is to our country and what a type of man he is." We then gave him a great cheer. I meant what I said about Kid Rock and he was by far the most popular single visitor that we had at Sather Air Base.

Two other visitors of note we had were from Fox News. The first was the war correspondent and Vietnam veteran, LtCol Oliver North. He was on his way to visit the U.S. Marines at Al Asad AB. Yet, I was able to talk to him for an hour or two about what we were doing at Sather and the conduct of the war. He took great interest in our first Chavis Turret and even got inside of it to test it out. He did some video on the turret but I knew that he wouldn't show it, he had really come to do a story on the marines in Iraq. He signed his name to our Virginia, State Street, barrier and left. The other visitor for Fox was the show host, Bill O'Reilly. I didn't know much about him and he seemed much like he was on the air, a bit of a curmudgeon. He also signed our State Street flag. Despite being a small base, we used the visits of our VIPs to the maximum extent possible for morale purposes and found that it worked well. While the Army looked on the VIP deluge as a nuisance, we were able to use it as a reward for good work.

Another program that we had initiated was building an intramural sports program for the base. When I arrived, and since it was the fall anyway, I asked for the Services Squadron to set up a flag football league. I had been on the flag football and softball team in Korea, so I saw this as a way to boost morale. It ended up exceeding all of my expectations. However, in the beginning, I got only the normal tepid response from Services, "We don't have a grass field, etc., etc.". I insisted that we could use the sand field for games and said that [447th] headquarters would field the first team, aptly named "the Geezers". All the big squadrons and even the Army unit fielded teams for the league, which played without pads or helmets and was low contact (sort of!).

The league started with 13 teams and began playing a couple games a night, which means that our Geezer team played every few days. It was great fun, with clouds of dust from the sand field, under the field lights. I played quarterback for the Geezers and spent most of my time running for my life. I forgot when I volunteered for that position that I would be playing against 18-20 year olds, who were playing for keeps. They chased me like I owed them money. The Geezers were "somewhat" competitive but only beat one team – the doctors and nurses of the base hospital. Since the Geezers were mostly old guys I didn't feel too bad about beating the hospital people up. Mostly though, we lost badly, but it was a for a good cause. Within a short time after the league started, the stands around the field were filled every night with fans from the 447th. It was like high school football night again except it happened several days a week. The league season lasted for almost two months and it certainly was a huge crowd-pleaser for the base. We even held playoffs with Civil Engineering winning the 447th Super bowl.

In addition to sandlot football, we had other sports leagues, like basketball, although I didn't participate in those. I knew that I had tempted fate with my football career and was happy to remain a spectator for the other sports. The point was that we made the most with what we had and it certainly raised morale with our various leagues.

As part of our "Make You Better" campaign, I had asked everyone in the camp to start various clubs or activities for the common good. I had done this at Bagram in Afghanistan to good effect. You never know what people were going to come up with. For instance, my deputy, LtCol Preston Smith, indulged his passion for star gazing by forming an astronomy club, using his own telescopes. Others formed activities that included video game players, bible studies and the like. I joined the "Weight Loss" class with about two dozen other people, which was taught by all the camp doctors. I was amazed at how good the instruction was and how much I personally learned in each weekly class. By way of instruction all of us in the class began to lose weight, which continued over the four-month period. Other classes taught by the hospital doctors included a "Stop Smoking" class and a "Pass the Physical Fitness Test (PFT)". We challenged people to come up with club and class ideas and they did so. I was excited to see how many responded to these classes. The point was that so many took our encouragement to improve themselves seriously during their time at Sather and did so. "Build it and they will come".

Another activity that originated from someone's creative thinking was a "Fire House Day" in September. It was a beautiful, bright day where squadron teams competed using various fire department events for the grand prize. Amazingly the "Geezers" team of five players finished second in the overall competition that included using a full-power fire hose, running with an empty fire hose and even putting on a fire suit, among other fire house activities. It was a rousing success and I personally got a great deal of enjoyment working with the firefighting gear. It was a really fun day and organized completely by CE and the fire unit for the pleasure of the other members of the 447th.

The logistics squadron organized another activity in January, based on a popular American television show called the "Great Race". Our Sather-based great race had teams running through the length of the entire camp from challenge to challenge. Once again, I participated and the Geezers lost out to the CE team for the top prize. My only disappointment was that some squadrons did not post teams because it was so close to the end of our tour. Still, it showed the ingenuity of our people to take the time to design and manage a base-wide course for this event.

Besides the mandatory 1.5 mile run/walk in Body Armor, the combat first aid classes and base-wide Operational Readiness Exercises (ORE's), I made one other contribution to the Sather activity picture. That was the start of "State Street". I asked all the base personnel to paint state flags on the 12' Alaskan concrete blast barriers on the street leading into the living area Sather. We called that road State Street. I requested that the Air National Guard people from my unit, the 111th Fighter Wing to paint the first barrier with the Pennsylvanian state flag. After we acquired some paint and brushes, the Pennsylvanian Guardsmen did so using a projector to trace the flag onto the barrier, then painted it by filling in the spaces. The next states were done by the big units in the 447th, but the project lagged for a short while. Then the spirit of Sather took over the project as people kept volunteering to do it after their work shift were finished. It was meticulous work but it kept getting done every night. The final push came from the hospital staff, under Colonel Dodson's vigorous guidance, who finished off the last 15 or so states. In the end, not only were all 50 states completed, but also

Puerto Rico and a few territories as well.

In the spirit of the monument that we had created, someone from Chicago wrote the city there and they sent an actual Chicago street sign that said "State Street" on it. We topped the sign off with several strands of barbed wire for the right "Sather" look and christened the street officially one night.

Below each state flag was a white area where each person from that state could sign their name with a permanent marker. One night we had the first signing of the flags by everyone in the 447th AEG – I signed under Pennsylvania. Once everyone had signed from the 447th, we invited all of our visiting VIPS to sign for their home state. However, by the end of the tour most of the signed names were beginning to fade completely and within another AEF tour they were gone. In retrospect, it is good that the names faded, but the extracurricular state flag painting workmanship of the 447th personnel lived on for future tours at Sather and is still there, I hope.

Another activity I continued from my command at Bagram, Afghanistan was to give out 447th AEG challenge coins to the top 10% performers in the unit. By this time in the war, all the commanders in the combat bases were giving out challenge coins to their best troops. I used the coins in a nice, formal ceremony. We would gather the few recipients in front of all their work mates, call out their names and give them the coin, a handshake and a salute. This was on top of the "shiny penny" program using the VIPs that I described earlier. I don't know what percentage other commanders used at their bases but I established the "10% rule" for Sather Air Base during our AEF tour. So, I ended up giving over 100 coins as a reward for great work.

I had said to our people that this would be the most important period of their lives. Now we needed to celebrate this fact.

The next morale program was *only done by us at Sather Air Base during our AEF tour*. It was my solution to the problem that I had identified upon arriving in Iraq, regarding the "percentage limit" on decorations given to personnel at Sather Air Base, as defined by BG Rand. I wanted us to have a celebration at the end of the AEF tour with a big morale event for deserving individuals – and we did. During this boisterous gala, we presented individual **Iraq campaign medals,** a personalized service certificate, a hand-shake from me, LtCol Smith and Chief MSgt Swarthout to every deserving individual in the 447th AEG, all before a raucous audience. Everyone was photographed by the public relations photographer receiving their certificate from me. All of the digital photographs were posted on the unit website so that they could be downloaded or printed by the individual.

The event was organized to provide the most excitement for each individual and was conducted as follows: twenty personnel would be grouped together to receive the Iraq Campaign Medal, with each awarded individually. We used the auditorium at the Glass House, which held about 100 seats, for this event and it was filled with friends and co-workers to wildly cheer everyone on. It was a very noisy and happy affair. An officer from their unit would call each member up to the stage. Then the officer would read three bullet statements citing their accomplishments, which had been drawn up by their unit commander. After those achievements were read, everyone would applaud and shout. I would pin on their decoration, present them with a certificate, followed by handshakes and salutes from our group leadership. Due to the large number of people in the 447th it took two weeks to hand out all the awards in this manner.

Normally, the vast majority of military personnel who receive the Iraq or Afghanistan campaign medals get them after they return to the U.S. with no fanfare, no fun, no personalized certificate, or a photograph with their commander. It just appears on a person's decorations list. We made it a big deal as our way of saying "thank you" at Sather Air Base for a job well done. Again, we were the *only* large military unit to perform this particular morale activity overseas.

The last morale activity we accomplished was a serious duty which demonstrated our spirit and commitment to our fallen comrades in Iraq at Sather Air Base. This activity was called the **Patriot Detail**. This was *the solemn transfer and guarding of the American coffins* as they were waiting to be transported from Baghdad back to the United States for burial. This was an activity manned solely by volunteers and managed and commanded by LtCol Preston Smith.

All the other bases in Iraq, including Balad Air Base, refused this ceremony, because it often involved meeting the flag-draped coffins in the early morning hours. In fact, BG Rand stated that unless each base met *every single coffin* that they would not be permitted to perform this solemn duty. LtCol Smith and his group of 30-40 steadfast volunteers made it happen. They ensured that each fallen hero was greeted and guarded by a group of volunteers in a formal ceremony while they were sitting at Sather Air Base. Often the caskets arrived with just an hour or two of notice in the early morning hours, yet these volunteers got up and were ready for the arrival of the coffins. LtCol Smith estimates that 80-85 coffins came through Sather Air Base during our tour and the Patriot Detail met every one of them. We were the only base that maintained this vigil during our AEF tour in Iraq during our AEF tour. We took good care of our fallen comrades while they were at Sather.

We sponsored a lot of morale activities and *I'm proud to say that most occurred only at Sather Air Base, during our AEF tour.* It just takes imagination and a little work to reward people for their hard work in a combat location. A prime example of this was the Iraqi Campaign Medal presentation, which capped off their tour, for almost everyone, with a happy memory of their deployment.

I believed then and still think now that we had the most innovative and expansive morale program of all the USAF and Army bases in Iraq during our AEF tour. It was a goal of mine to be the best in everything and we worked it hard to get there, as far as morale events go. Yet in the end, the U.S. Air Force would state that we were the worst, as you will see.

CHAPTER TWELVE
DEATH OF A TEAM

As the AEF tour neared the end, I was finding myself slowing down somewhat. Many of the major problems had been resolved and we settled into more of a routine. Yet, the daily pace was unrelenting and I have described only about 10% of the action in the AEF tour. There was a daily set of meetings, briefings, the huge number of email responses on both the NIPRnet, the unclassified email network, and SIPRnet, the classified email system. We had a large amount of taskings from Balad AB, covering a large number of topics, from the important to the ridiculous. I had to fill out a daily secret Situational Report (SITREP) on the status of Sather Air Base. I loved it all and derived a great deal of satisfaction from solving problems and making Sather better and safer. Yet, the untiring pace, with no days off for over four months was exhausting, both physically and mentally. I began to cut back near the end and limited myself to only 12-hour days. Personally, I had pushed very hard to solve the many issues at Sather Air Base. Furthermore, I had worked out daily in the gym (lifting weights) for my first three and a half months and had lost over 20 pounds of weight. But near the end of the deployment I had torn a muscle in my right infraspinatus (back shoulder) in the gym and I had to restrict my physical training program to simply walking a great deal every day. I was in some considerable pain from this muscle tear during the last month of the tour, but the doctors prescribed some mild pain medication to help.

As far as the 447th Group went, I continued to preach the mantra of maintaining the pace while also keeping it safe to the end. I spoke constantly of the dangers of the beginning and end of the tour, as I had briefed in the December 31st commanders call. I preached this at every staff meetings and in every public forum that I attended – keep focused and don't bend the rules for the sake of expediency.

After the day-long commander's call briefings on December 31, it was nice to have an outdoor New Year's Eve party near the Chaplain's coffee area. Many people stayed up that night to count down the time and we even had a lighted Civil Engineer-built "ball" dropped down from a crane as we ushered in the new year.

Of course, our New Year celebration was accompanied by the nightly gunfire from the nearby Iraqi special forces camp, which gave it the Sather AB "feeling".

Late in our AEF tour we had a visit from the USAF Chief Chaplain, a two-star general. Not a big event, since we had seen scores of other Major Generals over the deployment. But I decided to use the opportunity to show some love to the heroes of our AEF tour at Sather, the EOD squadron. Although we always put out notices to reward star personnel with our "shiny penny" initiative, I rarely, if ever, saw anyone from EOD in our group of challenge coin recipients. I decided to fix that deficiency with the two-star Chaplain by bringing the "shiny penny" general *to them*. We were going to take him directly to visit the EOD camp to shake hands and give out coins in their area. This was a 15-minute ride to get to the EOD camp, but when we got there only a couple people from the unit showed up. I had given them plenty of notice and warning about the general's arrival, but was irritated by the lack of EOD personnel coming to this event. I couldn't tell if the EOD personnel were all out at the Army FOBs or because they were simply blowing this event off. Every time I dealt with the EOD unit I felt a vague sense of arrogance and superiority from them and their leadership. I thought this was a dangerous combination in a combat area and in the end, I was right.

On the day when I was originally scheduled to leave Iraq, January 9th, I got the message that every commander dreads: we had personnel who were killed and wounded. The call came from the commander of the Civil Engineer unit, that oversees the EOD squadron. A team in the EOD unit had accidently set off an improvised explosive device (IED). LtCol Smith had written the names down of the personnel but we didn't do a good job of getting all the names down correctly. In retrospect, I should have been more careful to get it all right, but I was haunted by a powerful incident in my own military history.

In 1997, I was flying with five other A-10 pilots on Good Friday at Willow Grove Air Reserve Station, Pennsylvania. One crashed and was killed near the airfield and as the only ranking member of our unit left at the base on this holiday afternoon, I was tasked to tell his wife of the incident, alone, because no chaplain was available. Yet news of the accident hit the television channels within five minutes. The pilot's wife called me at the squadron and asked if it was her husband was involved in the A-10 accident. I already knew he had been killed and didn't want her to leave her home, so I gave her the best answer that I could think of at the time, "do you have someone home with you now?" She knew that he was involved in the accident and then screamed poignantly into the phone. Less than an hour later, I told her of the actual news of his demise, in person. The point of this story is that bad news travels very fast and we needed to get the notifications done quickly before they appeared on the internet or the television news.

Fast forward to 2007 and I called General Rand immediately with the news of the incident and the names of the individuals. Three EOD airmen were killed in action (KIA) and one was wounded. To put it in perspective, the USAF had only lost just 13 Airmen up to this point in Iraq. Yet, it pales in comparison to the total American servicemen lost in the Iraq war, since 2003, of over 4400 KIA.

So, began, what in retrospect, was one of the worst weeks of my life. I would make several crucial mistakes, as well as losing my cool, which would eventually cause me to lose my promotion to Brigadier General, which was only several months away.

After we found out the basics of the IED incident, I began to dig deeper. I wanted to know what happened because I always had an unsettled feeling about this EOD unit and now about this deadly event. The only surviving member of the USAF 447th EOD team provided the details to this *easily preventable* incident.

The unfortunate story began when a call came into an Army FOB about an empty civilian van sitting alongside a road that still had the engine running. The driver's door was open and inside the van was a pile of easily seen rockets. The EOD team, called "Team Lima" drove by the van in their heavily-armored Mine-Resistant, Ambush Protected (MRAP) vehicle. The MRAP had more armor protection than any other vehicle in Iraq except the M-1 Abrams tank. From the absolute safety of the MRAP, Team Lima looked into the van and could see rockets stacked in the interior. Team Lima's next procedure should be to move about 300 yards away from the van and to send an EOD Bot, a small, tracked, robot vehicle to more closely examine the vehicle. They could then use the Bot to place an explosive charge on the rockets and blow up the van and its deadly contents. No one would be hurt and another IED threat would be thwarted. Yet, for some unfathomable reason, that's not what they did. They took the most reckless and dangerous course of action possible. The entire team left the protection and safety of the MRAP vehicle, then surrounded the van and started to open its doors and the trunk. The trunk was booby trapped with a large, hidden bomb, which went off when it was opened. The only member of the team who survived the massive blast had stood near the shelter of the MRAP vehicle door and body. This incident was a violation of every rule that the EOD had shown me when I visited their building and operation in September. On that visit, the EOD personnel excitedly showed me how they used their EOD bots to disable or blow up IEDs. Yet they had *not* used them in this incident, with deadly results. There was nothing wrong with the EOD bots located with the Team Lima, they just hadn't used them.

I was angry when I realized what had happened with Team Lima and this unnecessary waste of lives. The bad guys had used a simple trick and our EOD team had fallen for it. Team Lima had done it right on 194 other occasions during this AEF tour, by destroying that number of IEDs. Now they disregarded their own EOD procedures and paid the price for their negligence. This was exactly what I had briefed to the 447th AEG in the commanders call – about getting overconfident and sloppy at the end of the AEF tour.

After the deadly IED incident, I cut off the unclassified internet connection from Sather Air Base to the United States, so that no one could notify the families of those killed or wounded via email or social media. The families were thus informed in the correct manner with a personal visit by an officer and a chaplain, of their loss without finding out beforehand.

Within several days of the IED explosion, BG Rand asked me to call the families of those killed and I did so. In a bygone time, the call or letter from the commander would have gone to the parents of the deceased. In the modern era, these young people, the oldest being

24, were raised by other many family members, such as grandmothers, etc. So, instead of making three total calls, I ended up making about eight or nine ones to various members of the deceased families. This was a mistake on my part and I should have just made the one call per person. But I erred on the side of compassion and it took a week to make all of these calls. I found them very depressing and personally I didn't feel like I did a good job soothing the loved ones. More than one person asked how they had been killed, but I was very careful to stay clear of saying anything about the actual incident. I simply told them that their loved one had died as a hero in service to a grateful nation. Still, these telephone calls to the loved ones really took a toll on me emotionally.

After a few days Balad's 332nd Wing launched a commander's investigation into the incident, as was required. I talked to the investigating officer myself and spoke my mind about the ridiculous mistakes made in this incident. The heart of the problem, in my opinion, was possible leadership issues in the EOD squadron. I told him about my concerns that members of the unit came across as arrogant, haughty and overconfident. The unit members had a superiority complex which caused them to reject their own procedures, leading directly to the death of three members of Team Lima. I was about to get a further dose of this attitude over the next week.

To my surprise, the 332nd AEW investigation into the incident simply ended. It was obvious that the USAF didn't want to examine this further or learn from these deadly mistakes. In USAF flight accidents, there is always an official investigation with findings and recommendations to prevent future problems in leadership or safety. Yet here, there was nothing. It was all just swept under the rug, which could lead to further deaths. So, I didn't let it go – a decision that would cost me in the end.

I started to talk to the overall commander of the Civil Engineering unit, Maj Robert Jones (not his real name). I asked Jones what he thought of the violation of the EOD procedures of this deadly incident. I got nothing. Up to now Jones had done a superior job, except for his significant pushback regarding the EOD clubhouse move after MG Holland's order to move the Fire / EOD units closer to safety at Sather Air Base. Was he afraid of EOD? Just because I was preaching to everyone at Sather to stay focused until the end of our tour didn't mean that others weren't getting "short". "Short" was the term we use in the military to describe the way people act when they only had a few days or weeks left in their tour. They start to "check out" mentally near the end of the deployment. Jones was definitely short and didn't want to deal with this issue. He gave me little feedback on the deadly EOD incident and nothing regarding any possible future fixes to their issues, if they had any.

I had been concerned about the attitude of the EOD personnel at Sather several times during this tour. They lived apart from the rest of the camp and spent most of their time on their own. They seemed to have a superiority complex because they were doing a dangerous job outside the wire. I checked the other Iraq USAF bases and Sather was the only one where the EOD lived separately outside of the main living camp. I was worried about them and where their attitude might lead.

I knew about people sometimes feeling superior, because I was a pilot. In my other AEF tours, in Afghanistan and Kuwait, the pilots had lived with the rest of the base population. We lived with them, showered with them, played volleyball with them and ate with them. We didn't portray ourselves as anything special, even though we were flying combat missions daily. The EOD airmen of the 447th did just the opposite, they lived separately, hung out with the army and presented themselves as something special. Their arrogance and attitude had now been a factor in getting them killed, in my opinion. Would more die now or in the future because of this attitude? I wanted to prevent that, which is why I continued to ask questions. I continued to pressure Jones to provide answers on this matter and genuinely wanted to hear what he thought. He continued to stonewall. Then came the incident that solidified my prior beliefs and ultimately ended my career prematurely.

About 10 days after the deaths of Team Lima we set up a memorial service. Rand called me before the ceremony and told me that he wanted the service to be no longer than an hour and for it to be "upbeat". I understood and concurred. He and his staff would also be there. Later that day I got a call from the Deputy Commander of the 332nd AEW at Balad. He reiterated that they wanted a short memorial service that was uplifting. I again concurred and said that we were going to model it after the service for Airman Chavis. I believe that I got one more call from Balad the next day, telling me to keep the ceremony short and upbeat. I understood and we made our plans.

Whenever we had a big visit from a general at Sather during this tour, we *always* conducted a full-dress rehearsal beforehand. We did so again for the memorial service. We began the rehearsal that morning, in preparation for the afternoon service. Shortly after the practice ceremony began, I delivered my entire "upbeat" speech, then sat down to hear the two EOD airmen who would give the final two speeches. But instead of the planned two, there were *six* speakers at the podium. I realized the EOD squadron was trying to add people to speak at the ceremony. I don't know if Major Jones was part of this little deception, but he did realize that they had been caught. Here I made a major error. Instead of punishing them and reducing the number of speakers, or keeping it to two persons only, I relented. I said that they could *all* speak if they kept their comments down to two-three minutes each. I then sat down to hear their speeches. They all said that their speeches were too emotional and that they couldn't give them without crying. They all asked not to give their speeches in front of me and my staff, because they said that they might start sobbing. I then made a second error. I said that if they gave their short speeches in front of the base chaplain, an officer, and CMSgt Swarthout then that was good enough for me. They all went off to practice their written speeches in front of those two people. Swarthout came back later and said the speeches sounded fine and short, as I had wanted. I made my third error and believed him.

Unfortunately, over my flying career, I had been to other memorial services for fallen pilot friends. I expected this ceremony to follow that pattern. Later that day, before the actual afternoon ceremony, I gathered the EOD speakers in a group and told them *again* that I wanted them to keep their speeches to 2-3 minutes each and to "tell me a [single] story of your [killed] friends, so everyone will care about them". They seemed to understand. I was influenced by the close friend of Airman Chavis, who had so moved me at his memorial. What we were about to get was a far cry from that ceremony or anything I had ever seen.

We started the afternoon memorial ceremony with about 500 guests in attendance. We filmed it for the families. At first, the ceremony went well, as we had practiced and it was running under the planned time of about 45 minutes. After giving so many prepared speeches this AEF tour, I thought that BG Rand and I gave pretty good addresses. I stated that Team Lima had dealt with 194 IEDs during their tour. I said that, "Team Lima had saved many lives in their dangerous profession to end the IED scourge in Iraq". I reiterated my call to SrA Elizabeth Loncki's [one of the airmen killed in Team Lima] mother. The mother had eventually asked me "what can I do for you and the people in Iraq?" I said that she had done enough with the loss of her only child. Still, the mother had baked some cookies and baked goods for us at Sather. I stated that, "This was the character of the people that we represent in the United States." I concluded with the following statement, "This is why we must continue to give our maximum effort at this critical time in this dangerous war." My speech was done in about six minutes.

Now it was time for the six EOD speakers to give their very short speeches and end the ceremony. What followed instead was a terrible travesty. The first EOD speaker gave his entire written speech instead of a shorter version. He went about 5-6 minutes. Then it went downhill very quickly. The next speaker was the most senior of the EOD group, a Staff Sergeant (E-5). About a minute into his speech he simply stated, "I'm not reading this damn speech, I'm going to talk as long as I want to." He then proceeded to ramble on for the next 20 minutes. He talked about getting drunk with Team Lima and doing tequila shots with them. He dropped the 'F-bomb" a couple times. This disjointed monologue was all being filmed for the Team Lima families! I was more than fuming, I was insanely upset. After he finished his rant the others continued in the same vein. Instead of taking a couple of minutes each, the EOD speakers vented on for over an hour. The 45-minute ceremony turned into a 90-minute one because of the EOD speakers. More than one talked about getting drunk with Team Lima. Instead of upbeat, poignant and short it morphed into a long, macabre and morose debacle. The EOD speakers rejected everything I had told them and went off script. It was the most disturbing memorial ceremony I had ever witnessed - *and it was all mine*. At the end of the ceremony I asked Swarthout about the speeches from the EOD people. He admitted that he and the chaplain had not listened to *any* of the speeches. He trusted the speakers to do as I ordered. BG Rand expressed his disappointment to me with the ceremony. I blubbered my intense apologies until he flew out of Sather. Then I went on the warpath.

I was insane with anger at that point. First the EOD squadron had spent the entire AEF tour acting superior, isolated and elite. Then three were killed and one wounded in an entirely needless and preventable IED incident. Then the EOD speakers had slipped in extra speakers when I was trying to be nice to them. They had purposely hidden their speeches from me because they were all going to say whatever they wanted. Then they rejected my instructions on keeping their speeches short and special. To my mind this unit was out of control and *rogue*. Would more be killed now or in the future because of this arrogance?

I went to my office with Swarthout and LtCol Smith and just seethed with anger. In retrospect, I should have cooled down and taken it slow. But I did not do so. I had a meltdown. I called in Maj Jones and his senior Civil Engineer NCO to my office. They were the direct supervisors of the EOD squadron. I asked them point blank whether they had been in on this little plan by the EOD speakers to highjack this ceremony. They said that they were not. I was breathing fire at this point. I cursed like a sailor and ranted. I asked him again whether he thought that there was a leadership or cultural problem with the EOD squadron? He again gave me nothing. In retrospect, I'm sure that he just wanted to go home and could care less about the EOD unit.

I remember saying to Jones that I wouldn't be around for his next AEF tour. He might even be in charge of an AEG group as the commander. What would he do then? I asked again and again, what should we do about the EOD unit? He said little, which just kept me hot. Finally, I let he and his NCO go. I didn't bring in the EOD squadron commander, a Captain, because I wanted this to be dealt with by Maj Jones. This was not about what the EOD people did but rather to discuss the symptoms of a rogue unit and how to fix it for the future. I wanted Jones to handle this issue and give me a recommendation on a course of action. He never did.

I brought in Maj Jones the next day and went hotly over my same arguments with him. Couldn't he see the danger in having a military unit filled with people who did whatever they wanted? This was how Team Lima was killed. I still got nothing from him. I retrospect, I believe that he just wanted to leave Iraq and avoid any investigation of the EOD unit that might stir up Inspector General (IG) complaints. So, Jones took a different tack. He had friends in the Pentagon and he used them.

Two days after the memorial service I was in the new DFAC, walking around and happily greeting tables of personnel as I liked to do in the morning. When I got to Maj Jones' table filled with CE personnel, he took me aside and then played me like a fiddle. He told me boldly that he had contacted the Pentagon, and a general that he knew, about my investigation of Team Lima. I was shocked, surprised and ranted in front of the CE people. I was still bent out of shape by the ceremony and lost lives. It wouldn't last. When I returned to my office I got a call directly from BG Rand. He asked me if I was still investigating the IED incident. I said yes. He told me to cease and desist on my own investigation AND to personally apologize to the EOD people. Major Jones had indeed contacted a Brigadier General friend in the Pentagon, as he told me in the chow hall, who had then contacted BG Rand. At the same time, CMSgt Swarthout was gently telling me in my office to, "Let this go."

Even though I believed that there was a real problem within the EOD unit, I did as instructed. I brought in Maj Jones, his senior NCO and all the EOD speakers at the Memorial Ceremony into my office and verbally apologized for my angry behavior and for launching my own investigation of the loss of Team Lima. I also went down to the EOD squadron and did the same sort of apology down there. I did so solemnly and with no sarcasm or vitriol. I did not curse or yell during these real apologies. I never did anything further concerning the deaths of the three EOD personnel, nor the speakers of the Memorial and just let it go. Nothing was ever learned from the death of Team Lima. Life went on and the transfer of personnel occurred at Sather Air Base at the end of AEF 3-4.

However, that didn't mean that I was done. As soon as the EOD squadron and Maj Jones finally left Sather to go home, I *immediately* went about fixing what I thought was the root cause of the problems with EOD. I told the *new* CE commander and my own replacement commander that *the new EOD unit <u>MUST</u> be moved immediately into the Sather camp* and live with the rest of the base population. I said further that the EOD squadron must be kept under tight reins or more would die. They both understood completely and moved the new EOD squadron personnel into the Sather base proper immediately after I left. My final problem was resolved and no further EOD airmen died needlessly from Sather Air Base.

My final question at the end of my tour was what to do about my written evaluation of Maj Jones. Originally, I had written Jones a stellar review and recommended him for one of the six "double" awards, i.e., two levels above the stated normal awards per person, for the entire Sather Air Base. I wrestled with this question until the day I left Sather Air Base. I was concerned about the fact that he had abdicated his responsibility to fix the dangerous issues that I saw with the EOD squadron. He gave me not one assessment or recommendation on how to correct the problems with them. Nor did he even acknowledge that there was trouble at all with this unit – even though needless deaths had occurred. He gave me not one bit of feedback on the EOD unit, their leadership or any issues with them. Doing great work for 90% of a deployment and then falling flat on your face for the final 10 yards didn't seem to justify a perfect review from me. I finally modified my overall review with the significant change of a single word from "exemplary" to just "good". I did not recommend him for a rare higher award, just the standard one for his rank. By doing so I sealed my own fate and incurred the wrath of someone who really knew how to use the system against me. The EOD issue and my handling of it would negatively affect my upcoming promotion to Brigadier General.

CHAPTER THIRTEEN
AFTER THE DEPLOYMENT - SUICIDE OF A COMRADE

After our long workdays were completed at Sather, almost every night, LtCol Smith, myself and CMSgt Swarthout would spend an hour or two on the roof of the Glass House, sitting on lawn chairs, smoking cigars, watching the delicate dance of aircraft and helicopters around Sather Air Base. We watched Saddam Hussein being off-loaded from helicopters during his trial, before he was hung by the Iraqi government in December 2006. We watched incredulously as one C-130 landed over 8,000 feet down the runway. Obviously, we had to debrief the pilot after that extremely poor landing that was caused by the fear of gunfire from Baghdad.

As time went on with these nightly gatherings, I became more and more philosophical. I mentored Smith and Swarthout particularly concerning the return to civilian life after the ultra-fast, high pressure pace that we held at Sather. I called the return home, after an extremely intense AEF tour, as equivalent to "falling off a bullet train" or "going from NASCAR racing to driving the family SUV - in one day". I found in my own experience, that the transition back to the civilian workplace and home life was particularly difficult. I did not know if they would have the same experience but tried to prepare them none-the-less. Swarthout was going to have a tough time due to his return as an executive for a tech company. I found out only recently that while Swarthout was in Iraq, his corporate job was being re-organized at home. This was a tactic used by certain employers to punish Reservists who deployed for many months overseas. U.S. federal law says that you can't fire a reservist because they deploy. But they still can "reorganize" the job, while the person is away. Swarthout evidently had several difficult, long-distance conference calls regarding just this sort of change, which undoubtedly added to his anxiety during our tour and when he returned home. Chief Swarthout and I finished our tour together at Sather Air Base and traveled thru Al Udeid Air Base, Qatar on the way back to the States. Al Udeid was much more pleasant on the way back home and we enjoyed our first beers there.

We continued all the way to Dover AFB, DE, where we split up. I shook his hand, thanked him for his service and his hard work at Sather Air Base, not knowing that I would never see him again.

The next time we talked, he called me at my home in Pennsylvania to complain about the excessive pressure that the IG was putting on him for negative anecdotes about me during our four-and-a-half-month AEF tour. I was shocked by the implications of this call, but did not fully understand its meaning then.

I then talked to Gordon again about six months later, when I invited him to my retirement ceremony in Pennsylvania. He seemed normal to me during our telephone calls. Sometime after that call, I mailed him a large, framed and happy picture of LtCol Smith, him, me and SrA Brabham all in the Glass House in Sather AB. About the time when he would have received that picture from me, he committed suicide.

I got word of the tragedy from his Air Force Reserve (AFR) commander at McCord AFB, Washington in 2008. The commander said that Swarthout had told his colleagues many good stories about his Iraq deployment, which again was his first and only combat tour. Gordon stated that he had learned many new leadership traits from me while in Iraq and was proud of our achievements there. But, the commander also said that Chief Swarthout had never been quite the same after he got back. Among other events, he became addicted to codeine, found in cough syrup, before his suicide.

I designed and mailed a personal, computer-made sympathy card to the Swarthout family, along with about two dozen pictures of him in Iraq. The family told his commander that these were the first pictures that they had seen of Gordon at Sather Air Base. My card was written from the heart and said, "I hope you know that Chief Swarthouts' work in Iraq saved lives". I further stated, "He touched many with extraordinary kindness and empathy…" I concluded it by saying, "It was an honor to become his friend".

The statistics show that, in 2016, over 20 American veterans commit suicide every day. A recent study shows that veterans are 18% more likely to commit suicide than the general population. The ratio is far higher if the veteran doesn't get help from the Veterans Administration (VA). I seriously doubt that Gordon got any assistance from anyone in the VA or otherwise. The macro view of suicide in the U.S.A. is that it is most prevalent among the 40-60 age group; then decreases until it again raises again in the 80+ age bracket. Gordon was in the "over 40" age bracket. Yet, these statistics are only real when it affects someone you know. At the time of his death, the suicide epidemic for returning Global War on Terrorism (GWOT) veterans was years from being recognized. I don't know why Gordon killed himself – his job, his life or whether he had PTSD and didn't get help. I don't know if the USAF IG investigation of my command at Sather may have affected his PTSD-troubled mind, but I wish I could have told him that my stalled promotion certainly wasn't worth his life.

After returning to the U.S. from Iraq, I became the Director of Operations of the Pennsylvania Air National Guard (PAANG), which means I was the deputy commander of over 4,500 ANG members. In March 2007, I got a call from my PAANG commander, Major General Steve Sischo. He said that the U.S. Senate had approved my general's list – the final step of a year-long process to get promoted to Brigadier General. Unfortunately, my promotion was being held up by an IG complaint. This was the first IG complaint I had ever received in 29 years. I was shocked to hear this news. That wasn't my only blow in 2007. For seven long months, I waited to hear what the USAF IG complaint was about. I was called in October 2007 by the Lt General in charge of the USAF Inspector General service. There were five charges against me. I was charged twice with creating a hostile environment and also with maltreating subordinates at the 447th AEG in Iraq. They were the same crimes since they concerned public profanity, yelling and personal and malicious public verbal assaults. I was also charged with three counts of abuse of authority and reprisal. These were serious charges and they certainly were an attempt to end my career and promotion. It's the old adage of "throwing as much jello against the wall and hoping that some of it would stick". Now I knew what this was about and who launched the IG attack against me; it was from Major Jones, the Civil Engineer commander.

The USAF IG complaint system is a formal structure built within the USAF/AFR/ANG to handle charges made against more senior ranked personnel. Every single complaint against a senior ranked individual must be investigated and one can make as many charges against a person as one wants. It is a bit like the tort system of the United States – you can sue anyone as many times as you like, with no ramifications for the one making the complaints. Plus, all complaints are held in confidence, so you never know who launched the investigation against you. Some of the more egregious charges that make the USAF IG headlines are cheating the government out of money, accepting bribes, sexual fraternization and sexual harassment.

Most of the IG complaints I saw in the Air National Guard were far more mundane. Let's take a typical case that I had seen used against other commanders. Airmen X, Y and Z are all applying for the same job or position. Commander A chooses Airman X for the job, based on performance. Airman Y and/or Z now can charge Commander A with discrimination regarding the job choice based on sex, age, race, ethnicity, sexual orientation or a combination of the above. Commander A doesn't know who charged him and must prove that he/she didn't do what was alleged. Commander A may be charged scores of times in his/her career for various IG "offenses". Although most charges are found as "unsubstantiated" it only takes one guilty verdict to ruin a career. When I asked my active duty counterparts at Balad how many times that they had been charged under the USAF IG complaint system, more than a few commanders said that they had been investigated between *40-50 times per person*. That's forty to fifty separate IG investigations. I was shocked because I had never had even one investigation.

Why had Major Jones made so many charges against me? It defies logic to make five substantial IG charges against someone because they yelled at you in a couple of private office visits. He made the charges because he did not get the medal award, a Bronze Star, that he wanted for this tour and because I had given him an average Letter of Evaluation (LOE). Jones had told me personally on several occasions that he had wanted a Bronze Star for his tour. Although I had originally thought to recommend Jones for a Meritorious Service Medal (MSM), one step down from the Bronze Star, I had decided against it after a long debate with myself and CMSgt Swarthout during the very last days of my tour. I still recommended him for a USAF Commendation Medal anyway, which he received, just not the one he wanted. BG Rand wouldn't have approved the Bronze Star, even if I had recommended it, because it was too far above his original parameters. Jones didn't get what he wanted, so he threw the book at me, in an attempt to ruin my career, with these IG charges. My own actions following the EOD deaths and the memorial ceremony had provided him with the necessary ammunition.

Looking back, some parts of the IG complaint system seemed rigged against the defendant. My investigation took 18 months, which meant that I could not appeal it, since my 30-year military tenure was over. Did it really take that long to do the investigation or did they just drag it out so that I couldn't petition it for another review, essentially an appeal? I could never find out because that's the way the system is set up.

Another unique aspect of the military IG system is that the defendant gets questioned by the investigating personnel with no lawyer present. In my case, I was interrogated by two Judge Advocate colonels by myself. An accompanying lawyer might have asked a few questions, like these, before my interview:

- What was the threshold of my crime, i.e., was one profane word too much?

- Were the circumstances of the deaths of Team Lima, the many calls to the families, or the horrible memorial ceremony mitigating factors?

- Is combat service over a long period of time a mitigating issue?

For seven months I floated in limbo, not even knowing what the charges were against me. Once charged I began to draw up a written defense to the charges. At least here I was able to do so with the advice of an ANG JAG (Judge Advocate) from my old A-10 unit. In retrospect, I should have engaged a top-end civilian lawyer with IG and UCMJ experience to handle my case. I was an IG newbie, with no prior investigations or charges against me, facing the entire USAF IG machine. Today, I compare my representation and advice as if I was flying a World War I biplane like the Nieuport SPAD S. versus the modern-day F-15C Eagle - I was totally out-manned, out-flown and out-mauevered. My appointed, paltry ANG lawyer certainly had no experience in this sort of combat-related, high-profile case. I should have realized that this may not be a fair investigation, when Chief Swarthout called me to complain of the IG investigators trying to force him to provide negative information on my command at Sather. He told me that they threatened him with punitive action toward *his* career unless he provided them with any specific negative instances of profanity, anger or yelling during the four and a half months of my combat command. It wasn't a review of my combat leadership but rather a witch hunt.

In January, 2008 I was given my only personal interrogation by the USAF IG. The interview lasted four hours. In the beginning, I was asked to present my view of the AEF 3-4. In retrospect, I should have questioned my interrogators apparent lack of combat experience, due to their lack of medals on their uniform. My investigators could not have served on a combat tour, because they didn't have the medals to show that. I had more medals than both of them put together. Then, I should have given a Power Point briefing on the unique aspects of our tour, especially as it applied to morale features. I did not address those nearly enough in my verbal description. Only at Sather Air Base did we have morale activities such as presenting the Iraqi Campaign Medal, a Sather Certificate signed by me, reading out of their achievements and a photograph with me all in a celebratory manner. Only at Sather did we use the VIP deluge to present hundreds of "shiny penny" challenge coins to our worthy recipients. Only at Sather did we train our personnel to the highest standards in combat first-aid and four Operational Readiness Exercises. Only at Sather did we have a flag football league, Fireman's Day and a contest for the "Great Race". Only at

Sather did we build a slew of programs to help everyone make themselves better. How did I know that we were unique in our programs at Sather Air Base? Because I heard from the other Group and Wing Commanders in Iraq on their base programs, when BG Rand held a commander's conference in Balad in October, 2006. Sather was alone in many of our morale programs, which is why I was distressed when accused of a hostile environment a year after the fact. In retrospect, I did not present our unique morale programs at Sather very well to the IG interrogators, but I seriously doubt if my programs would have made any difference. After two hours of talking about the positive aspects of the Sather AEF tour we took a break and they started to get into the individual negative events of the deployment.

Since I admitted to the profanity in my office following the memorial ceremony they centered on the meltdown I had at the chow hall. Since this event was a little hazy to me, at the time of the interview, they really keyed on it. But I really missed an opportunity to put this isolated event into perspective, since it happened at the end of a long, stressful AEF tour, after the death of Team Lima, talking to the Team Lima families and the failed memorial ceremony all occurring in under a two-week period.

As far as the post-memorial meltdown in my office with Major Jones, I admitted to those incidents then and now. These were in two private meetings was just with two people and my chow hall profanity was heard by just one table of CE people. Yet, after these events I also gave several heartfelt apologies to all those concerned. On the other hand, I had literally hundreds of private meetings and public speeches in Iraq where no profanity or harsh language was used. 97% of those in my command never heard me use profanity or yelling. The people who did hear something were given a personal apology within a day or two of the event. I was not a General Patton-type who used profanity in public talks to those in his command – that was not my style. Yet, the IG was seeking any and every profane statement I ever made and then amplifying that into a general mode of behavior and negative leadership quality.

I asked a living member of my staff, LtCol Preston Smith, a decade after the event, about the level of pressure that he experienced from the IG concerning my case. He said the amount of coercion was very high to provide any negative examples of my leadership behavior. He expressly used the word "witch hunt" to describe the investigation. Not a balanced view of my leadership but a search for anything negative. As with Swarthout, the IG investigators also threatened him with negative career actions if he didn't give them something bad.

Another aspect of the David vs. Goliath struggle with the USAF IG complaint system was the fact that I was in the Air National Guard. I believe the system was biased and my ANG-fueled preparation was very poor. When I went to the Army National Guard IG personnel from my headquarters unit at Fort Indiantown Gap, PA in 2007 for advice, they gave me, in hindsight, extremely unsound guidance - everything they told me was wrong. Since this was my first IG complaint, I was a neophyte. For instance, they advised me to wear the new USAF fatigues, Airman Battle Uniform (ABUs) instead of my Class A blue uniform, with my medals, to my interrogation. It looked as if I didn't take this investigation seriously enough with my ABU's on. They gave me no instructions on how to present my case to the IG. As I said, I should have presented the IG inspectors with a formal briefing of the many positive, progressive aspects of Sather Air Base, instead of trying to wing it with a verbal description.

Did I use profanity in my four and a half months of deployment? Yes. Did I use profanity as a leadership method or tool? NO! I profoundly reject that allegation on either a micro or macro level. I provided a positive, uplifting leadership style in public and private. I had literally hundreds of speeches, talks, presentations, meetings and conversations in public and private where no profanity occurred. The overwhelming majority of the personnel in the 447th never heard even *one word of profanity* from my mouth. Yet isolated incidents were extrapolated into a general mode of profane and negative operations that never existed.

Why did the USAF IG put so much pressure on people to provide negative isolated incidents for the investigation? My assertion is that the USAF and IG had already decided that I was guilty and they wanted to make an example of me. Major Jones had great support in the USAF and convinced the IG that my command was the worst form of profane-based blasphemy.

The civilian leadership of the Department of Defense, led by Secretary of Defense Gates, wanted to eliminate the hard-charging, cigar-smoking, fighter pilot generals. I was in the Air National Guard, with no support in the Pentagon or USAF, so it was easy to dispose of me. There was no discussion or questions concerning the achievements of the 447th of the AEF tour. That didn't matter. What they wanted was a perfect leader, in the politically correct Air Force. It was more important to *never* say a bad word than to achieve anything. If you said a profane word *once* then that must have been your general operating strategy. Further, my investigators had not served as commanders in Iraq or Afghanistan and did not know the pressures and challenges of that position. It is easy to judge when you have not experienced it for yourself.

Ultimately, I was found guilty by the U.S. Air Force twice for "public profanity, yelling, and personal and malicious public verbal assaults". Why I was convicted twice for exactly the same crime (public and private profanity) is unknown to me. Other general officers had been promoted after a single IG finding, but not two. So, this IG report killed my promotion. I was retired out of the ANG within a week. I find it very suspicious that this investigation took one and a half years, which is exactly as long as I had left in my career as a Colonel. I was told, on my last day of my career, that if **I didn't go to the press** with this, the USAF would also keep it quiet. My regret now is that I didn't take this to the "Air Force Times" or other media outlets. A real press investigation into our AEF 3-4 tour at Sather Air Base would have exposed the hypocrisy of this so-called investigation, that was focused only on the negative and not on any of the positive events and combat leadership style that I used at Sather. I did not go to the press, then, because I had just had my first spinal surgery for a back injury incurred during an A-10 flight in 2004. I was too devastated by the pain from that surgery to focus on a press-nurtured counter-attack.

In a press campaign, I would have admitted to the two meetings of profanity with Major Jones and for the yelling for a minute in the Sather DFAC. Yet within a day of those regrettable events, all occurring within a 48-hour period, I apologized to all those concerned.

Nothing was said in the IG report of the extraordinary efforts we made at Sather to boost morale. There was nothing about all of the upbeat aspects to our life at Sather, because of our unit's positive attitude. For instance, Major Jones personally received from me a 447th AEG challenge coin in a public event, an Iraq Campaign Certificate and medal from me in a high energetic public ceremony and a USAF Commendation Medal recommendation from me. I honestly felt that the AEF tour at Sather Air Base was a great experience for the vast majority of the Airmen, Army, Brits and civilians. Because we left the base and our people in far better shape than when we received it. Our personnel had been excited about the great things that they had accomplished. I had provided positive language in my leadership. Yet, the report from the IG makes it seem like I was the worst tyrant, someone who abused and threatened his airmen on a daily basis.

The US Air Force IG spent 1 ½ years focusing on my minor, hot-tempered errors during an intense, combat AEF tour which lasted 4 ½ months long with not one day off. However, nothing was studied or published on how and why three highly-experienced USAF EOD technicians made basic "rookie mistakes" that ended up costing them their lives in a needless and preventable IED incident. In the end, it was only my efforts, after Major Jones had departed Sather Air Base, that changed the leadership parameters for the 447th EOD squadron and prevented future casualties there.

While dealing with the pain from my back surgery in the summer of 2008, I was mentally crushed by the findings of the USAF IG. However, on every other front, except the IG, the 447th AEG did well. After the AEF 3-4 tour, the 447th AEG was awarded with the *Meritorious Unit Award by the U.S. Air Force.* This is a high award for a unit in combat. I was personally awarded by the USAF with a *Bronze Star for achievement.* I received a glowing and perfect *Letter of Evaluation* for my time at Sather from BG Rand. BG Rand gave me a powerful personal sendoff from Sather on my last day of command there. The third and final version of the Chavis turret came out only months after our second prototype, in the Spring of 2007.

The newest Chavis turret was manufactured into the USAF standard for the entire Iraq and Afghanistan theater and over 60 were made. No further turret gunners were killed with this new model for the Air Force.

On my last day of service in the USAF and the Air National Guard, my boss, MG Sischo, said, "I know you are disappointed not to be promoted to Brigadier General. But it was far more important for you to go to Iraq to do the good things you did there." He was right, and that's what this book has been about. It was a highlight of my professional career and I'm glad I volunteered to go there.

EPILOGUE

The purpose of this book is to share my experiences in providing proper leadership in a dangerous combat environment. A subject that I have avoided so far is why I thought the prior commanders at Sather missed and/or did not deal with the many hazardous issues at Sather Air Base during their tours. Why did over a dozen prior commanders, spanning three and a half years, overlook or neglect the critical issues that were discovered and corrected in AEF 3-4? They weren't lazy or stupid but I can narrow the answer to several reasons that I will now discuss. The first reason why these dangerous issues weren't dealt with by prior commanders at Sather was because of the **lack of continuity** by commanders, caused by the short length of the USAF AEF tour, which, at the time, was four months. I was fortunate to have spent seven months commanding Bagram Air Base, Afghanistan, prior to my Sather deployment. That Afghanistan tour certainly prepared me, as nothing else could have, for what I was going to experience at Sather. I was able to anticipate events at Sather rather than just react to them. My experience commanding two different combat bases was what led me to tell Lt Gen North during my Christmas Day, 2006 briefing, before we dedicated the chow hall DFAC, that I thought that the current AEF tours were too short for commanders and their staffs. During my Sather and Bagram deployments, it took over 2-3 months just to make personal contacts with other service commanders necessary to resolve many of the base's issues. I recommended to North that the optimum AEF tour length for USAF commanders be six months, similar to the length of the USMC combat deployments, which were seven months in length. Six months would provide commanders and their staff enough time to identify all the base and personnel issues, then work to effectively resolve them, while not being so long as to deplete their energy level. Six months would force those personnel to focus on the deployment versus just trying to glide through the tour. Conversely, a year-long deployment turns into a much longer marathon and forces the commander to lower his/her daily vitality level to survive that length of a tour. I know this to be true because I had done a one year tour in Korea as an OV-10 pilot. The second reason for setting the AEF tour to six months was to allow AF Reserve and Air National Guard leaders to volunteer for commander positions.

In my opinion, I don't think that reservists would volunteer for a year-long tour. Allowing reservists to apply for the commander and deputy commander positions in the combat leadership jobs in the USAF enables them to offer their unique perspective for these jobs. Not to disparage my active duty senior-ranked brethren in Iraq and Afghanistan, but I felt that the reservists offered a more experienced viewpoint than their younger active duty counterparts. Additionally, they were all volunteers and generally reservists were more willing to take risks toward solving complex issues.

At some point after 2007, CENTAF changed the tour length for the geographically-separated base commander positions, such as those I held at Sather AB and Bagram AB, to one-year tours. This effectively ended the experiment of using reservist volunteers for those critical jobs. Still, the four-month tour length wasn't the reason that Sather's dangerous and complex problems weren't solved previously. The short tour length just gave the prior 447th AEG commanders an excuse for not dealing with its problems.

The main reason that perilous issues at Sather weren't addressed for three and a half years was because the previous commanders were what I call **minimalist leaders**. *A minimalist leader is a commander or CEO who takes the path of least resistance and minimizes any risks to their career during their tenure.* They're more interested in preserving their career than doing the best job for their organization or company. They fail to investigate potential problem areas and generally incur the smallest amount of danger to their career path in a "cruise through the tour" mentality. USAF commanders often inherit well maintained organizations when they come into their leadership role, which along with the short length of this tour, allows this sort of *risk aversion* command behavior. Sather Air Base did not, on its surface, present itself as a dangerous place. If I had not done the base-wide inspection and other investigations, I might not have discovered the vulnerabilities dangers inherent of the base. But I knew I needed to do the inspection because of my Bagram experience. My prior command tours had showed me that the base inspection was the most efficient and quickest way to find any problem areas and to get to know one's people. I did the inspection because I wanted the 447th AEG to help us win the war, not just to obtain another successful milestone in my career.

My predecessor said, during my changeover, that Sather Air Base was in good shape and I could have taken his word for it. I could have performed as the prior minimalist leaders and just glided through my tour to collect my Iraq medal and promotion at the end. Most likely the dangers in the Sather air traffic system, the security issues, the rocket attacks, etc. would not have caused any fatalities during my tour. We still would have done a good enough job during my tour by taking the path of least resistance. Yet, I discovered dangers and was not going to just sit by while they festered.

The minimalist leader can sink their unit or company, because, by minimizing their own command problems, they put the overall organization at risk. If the anti-government forces in Iraq had been able to launch a raid against Sather Air Base from BIAP before we fortified the base and practiced for an attack; or if an Army helicopter had collided with an USAF cargo plane loaded with troops before we fixed the ATC system, hundreds of American servicemen could have been killed and wounded. The enemy would have scored a huge public relations victory for little cost or effort.

The minimalist leader works hard to appear to be doing well while minimizing his/her own career risk. Sather's large number of prior commanders made me initially assume that the base would be in good shape. In contrast, because Bagram AB, Afghanistan was a new base, I knew that there would be many issues to resolve and I went there with that mindset. I believe that these prior commanders at Sather had been applying a peacetime USAF "business as usual" mentality toward a wartime situation. They had assumed that because this was the way it had been done before at Sather AB, that it could just continue that way. Since neither the 447th individual squadrons nor their subordinates didn't raise any issues, then the situation must be fine. This exemplified the "ask no questions and make no waves" mentality of the minimalist leader. I think that the IG oversight of commanders in the USAF has neutered many commanders so much that the form of the operation is frequently more important than the content of it.

Being promoted into the higher ranks in the USAF is often not so much about creative thinking as a commander, but surviving the gauntlet of potential negative events thrown in your path, as well as having a high-placed mentor to help your career. As the prior commanders at Sather showed, it's about risk aversion. You must pass every USAF IG ORI (Operational Readiness Inspection), have no aircraft accidents or sexual harassment, have no personal or unit IG complaints that stick to you. Generally, you will find that most high-ranking generals in the USAF had *minimized their time as commanders*, because that's where they are vulnerable to all these negative events that can destroy a career. For instance, being a Squadron Commander of a high-risk fighter squadron for one year, versus three years, counts the same toward fulfilling the commander "block" while abating any of these career-ending events by two-thirds. So, the career-conscious "fast burners" *minimize* their command time. The USAF system is set up to punish severely any negative events, regardless of how many positive things you may have accomplished. So, the overall tendency for those whose primary concern is promotion is to keep your head down and do the minimum required to survive. The prior commanders at Sather took the least possible risk which meant supporting the status quo.

Let's face it, in an atmosphere of career-ending negative consequences, it is far easier to cruise through the job, make no waves, upset no one, and just call it good. In an environment of risk aversion, a hard-charging commander must be willing to do the right thing regardless of the consequences, if he/she wants to achieve results. That's why I found so many egregious leadership sinkholes during my tour at Sather. For instance, why people went hungry for over three and a half years was just an issue beyond my comprehension as a commander - a gross oversight. The issues concerning protection of the base personnel from rocket attacks is also tough for me to understand. Perhaps as the Iranians brought more rockets into Baghdad (thru BIAP) this increased the number of rocket attacks against Sather. Still, I know that Sather previously had been slammed by rockets before, because one scored a direct hit on a 10,000-gallon fuel bladder, burning it in a huge fireball. That burn hole was still at the base when I arrived, acting like a warning beacon toward potential future rocket attacks. With that knowledge, as a commander, you have to prepare the base and your people for that threat. I built up the fortifications and gave ORE training preparation at Bagram Air Base, Afghanistan, during my tour, when we were hit by just *one* rocket. Sather's high number of rocket attacks had to be addressed. Yet when I arrived at Sather there were *no* bomb shelters, no litters, no first aid kits, no casualty recovery system, no training, nor were there enough blast barriers.

The air traffic control issues at Sather and the security issues in the Baghdad tower were, along with the food issue, the greatest oversight of the prior commanders. It wasn't just one problem but a plethora of them – any of which could have cost hundreds of American lives or given the enemy an enormous propaganda victory for no cost. In the end, it's all about creating a Warrior Ethos for yourself as the commander and for your people. A Warrior commander doesn't allow his/her people to go hungry or live in needless danger.

I have always been a risk-taker and I took many gambles to make things better at Sather Air Base. Partly it was based on my experience as commander of Bagram Air Base, Afghanistan and it also was my desire to genuinely help win the Iraq War. As I look back a decade later on my performance in Iraq, I certainly would have changed some things, if I had to do it over again. But you can't create that much modification and fix that many serious, dangerous issues without pushing the system pretty hard. I would have also dialed back my hot temper a notch or two. I deeply regret my profane incidents. But I went there to win and fix things is exactly what I did. For three and a half years many severe problems went unaddressed because of feckless and ineffective leadership at Sather Air Base. We won the race to keep the enemy from discovering the weaknesses there and to stop a tragic accident from killing many of our servicemen. Either event would have been a defeat that could have helped turn the public against the war. Hardworking Sather Airmen went hungry and they were in mortal danger, even if they didn't know it.

A decade later, the only thing that matters is that we saved lives at Sather Air Base then and into the future. I am bothered to this day that I had not picked up on the distress in Gordon Swarthout's life and somehow could have helped him. As far as the IG investigation goes, I look back on a process that was warped to end my career. I've since read that the new Secretary of Defense in 2006, Robert Gates, wanted to diminish the number of hard-charging generals who had emerged from the fighter pilot culture and had been the darlings of prior promotion boards. My quiet sacrifice, with minimum publicity, was a message to all concerned that profanity, no matter the circumstances, was not going to be tolerated in the new USAF/ANG. I had been found guilty from the beginning and nothing I said or demonstrated by my performance was going to change that judgement.

We made significant changes during our AEF tour due to the hard work of the people of Sather Air Base during AEF 3-4 in 2006-7. I was proud to lead that unit then and am still happy now to have been given this wonderful opportunity to have been part of the storied 447th AEG.

I am often asked how the youngest generation performed during my tours in Iraq and Afghanistan. How did the "millennials" stack up against prior generations in a combat environment? They performed magnificently, as young American volunteers have done over the last 240 years of war. Their youthful spirit was contagious and a pleasure to behold and lead. They were the best. The millennials did very well indeed.

FINAL NOTE: In 2011, in front of the Glass House at Sather Air Base, Secretary of Defense Panetta, in President Obama's administration, declared the Iraq War won and the task completed, then departed the same day from Sather. Of course, they ignored the American history of rehabilitating dictatorships in Japan, Germany and South Korea. Tasks that took a generation or more to complete, not just 8 years. That gross error meant that every US servicemen's death was in vain and led to the formation of ISIS and the loss of 40% of Iraqi territory to that caliphate. The U.S. military had to re-enter Iraq to complete the rehab of Iraq in 2014 and will be there for many years to come. Sather Air Base now belongs to the Iraqi Air Force.

I thank you reader for taking the time to hear this tale. I hope that you were entertained and that you will be inspired by the fact that many young Americans continue to perform great things in the service to our country. My final words are what I had the WWE wrestlers and airmen shout as we stood under the dome of the Glass House near Christmas in 2006. "**AIRPOWER!**"

The End

ACKNOWLEDGEMENTS

This book is dedicated to the real heroes: those in the 447th AEG, Iraq and 447th Bomb Group, England (WW II) that didn't make it back home to their families and loved ones.

I would like to recognize my two editors who worked tirelessly with me over many months to bring this version to you. The first was Colonel Thomas Lytle (USAF, ret) who corrected my military facts and helped with the heavy editing. He was also there for moral support when the going got tough. Bob Staranowicz came on later in the process but also was there in the final editing effort. I thank them both for making this book what it is today.

I want to thank the men and women who served with me in the 447th Air Expeditionary Group (AEG) during AEF 3-4 in 2006-7, who I wasn't able to acknowledge in this book. As I said to my airmen, their time in Iraq would be the highlight of their professional lives – and it was. Being at a combat base was an intense experience for the Airmen, Army, British and civilians of Sather Air Base. A commander is only as good as his people and the vast majority who worked for me gave it everything they had during their tours. They believed in the missions as I defined them and worked 12-18 hours a day, every day, to make it happen.

Some of the Air Force personnel were volunteers for this tour, including 33 members of my Air National Guard unit from Willow Grove, PA, the 111th Fighter Wing. First, they had to volunteer to be in the Air Guard, then to volunteer again to go with me to Baghdad. They offered to accompany me on this tour and did so. They deserve my sincere and special gratitude. All of them came to an environment that tended to look down upon the reserve members of the military. Yet they overcame these prejudices and demonstrated their leadership brightly in the form of the Chavis turret and many other successes.

I finally want to thank my commanders Lt General North and Brigadier General Rand for their support during my tour. I didn't always make all the right choices but they let me fix most of the issues as I saw them at Sather Air Base. I was fortunate to arrive at the tipping point for the Iraqi conflict, where it could have moved toward victory or toward another Vietnam. Leadership is about setting tasks for your people and having them execute them. 99% of the personnel at Sather Air Base worked diligently to make their tour a brilliant triumph and they have my unending gratitude.

Unveiling of the Chavis Turret, Version 1 (left) with the old, inadequate USAF turret on the right Humvee

Sather Air Base with the Glass House Headquarters building in the background

447th AEG Headquarters Staff for AEF 3-4
next to the glass dome of the Glass House,
showing various rockets shot at the base during this tour

Pep Talk before the Body Armor Run on
October 1, 2006

Combat First Aid Instruction and Practice
September, 2006

Casualty Care in a Nighttime Exercise

Col Marston and Lt Gen North during his first Sather visit in Oct, 2006

Firehouse Day, Oct 2006

Speech before the opening of Cheyenne's Grill, the self-made chow
hall serving the first meals at Sather AB in 3 ½ years

Aircraft on Sather flight line and the first stop for many soldiers into Iraq. Sather was the #1 passenger entry point into Iraq at that time

Airmen huddled in new bomb shelters on the last no notice, night-time practice exercise in November, 2006

.

Briefing by Col Marston in Glass House while wearing body armor

Meeting Secretary of State Condoleezza Rice after she had a security delay of 30 minutes

The BIAP Tower where so many serious security and air traffic
control problems were discovered

Shrapnel hole in a C-5A aircraft from a rocket attack in December, 2006. The damaged aircraft limped out of the base the next day with over 30 holes in it

Col Marston with singer Kid Rock on Christmas Day, 2006. Kid Rock was the airmen's favorite visitor during the tour

Lt Gen North with the builders of the Chavis Turret on Christmas Day, 2006

Chavis Turret, version 2 in Jan, 2007.It was immediately tested under combat conditions in Baghdad with an USAF Security Forces unit – and they loved it

Col Marston with some of the Pennsylvanian Guardsmen who accompanied him to Sather AB,in front of State Street

A unit member receives her Iraq Campaign Medal and serving certificate in a happy ceremony in Jan, 2007. The 447th AEG was the only unit to do this ceremony in Iraq